My Kind of Transit

My Kind of Transit

Rethinking Public Transportation in America

DARRIN NORDAHL

The Center for American Places
at Columbia College Chicago

in association with
The Elizabeth Firestone Graham Foundation

The Center for American Places at Columbia College Chicago
600 South Michigan Avenue
Chicago, Illinois 60605-1996, U.S.A.
www.americanplaces.org

Distributed by the University of Chicago Press
www.press.uchicago.edu

16 15 14 13 12 11 10 09 08   1 2 3 4 5

Library of Congress Cataloging-in-Publication Data

Nordahl, Darrin.
  My kind of transit : rethinking public transportation in America / by Darrin Nordahl. -- 1st ed.
      p. cm. -- (My kind of transit ; v. 30)
  Includes bibliographical references.
  ISBN 1-930066-88-0 (acid-free paper)
  1. Local transit--United States—Case studies. 2. Urban transportation—United States—
Case studies. 3. Local transit—United States—Social aspects. I. Title. II. Series.

 HE4451.N67 2008
 388.40973--dc22

                               2008035711

ISBN-10: 1-930066-88-0
ISBN-13: 978-1-930066-88-5

Frontispiece: The funicular in Pittsburgh, Pennsylvania.
All photographs are by the author, except as otherwise noted.

To Noe, Nate, and Mia

CONTENTS

THE ICONIC *STAR FERRY*, HONG KONG'S OLDEST FORM OF PUBLIC TRANSIT, OFFERS BREATHTAKING
VIEWS OF THE CITY'S SKYLINE AND VICTORIA PEAK. IT IS OFTEN SAID THAT ONE CANNOT TRULY
EXPERIENCE THE MAGIC OF HONG KONG WITHOUT A TRIP ACROSS THE HARBOR AT TWILIGHT.

This book offers a different perspective on public transportation in the United States. The focus here is neither the economical nor environmental benefits of public transit travel (of which there are many) but the experience offered to the passenger and onlooker. I wish to show that, through thoughtful planning and design, the transit vehicle—a mobile form of public space—can provide a setting for public life and thus enrich many aspects of our everyday lives.

In my travels around the world, I have always relied on public transportation to shuttle me to various points of interest within each city. It was in Hong Kong where I realized that public transportation is not just a means to a destination but a destination itself. Consult any guidebook of the city and one will find Hong Kong's public transport systems are points of interest: the engineering marvel of the nineteenth-century funicular that climbs and descends the precipitous face of Victoria Peak; the *Star Ferry* (also a product of the nineteenth-century), which offers magical views of the city's skyline from Victoria Harbor; the sheer length of Central's pedestrian escalator (the longest in the world); and the brightly colored double-decker trams that course through the bustling streets of the island. I have come to recognize that my fondest memories of Hong Kong, and many of my most joyful experiences, were fostered aboard these compelling transit systems. Within Hong Kong's diversity of unique transit vehicles, I was able to connect to the larger

THE CENTRAL ESCALATOR IS HONG KONG'S NEWEST AND MOST UNUSUAL FORM OF PUBLIC TRANSIT. IT
TAKES TWENTY MINUTES FOR COMMUTERS TO COMPLETE A TRIP FROM THEIR RESIDENCES IN THE
MID-LEVELS DOWN TO THE SKYSCRAPERS BELOW, PASSING RESTAURANTS, BARS, AND SHOPS ALONG
THE WAY.

landscape, discern the historical development of the city, converse with locals, and, hence, learn more about this unique culture and place. I concluded: if such enriched experiences could be had aboard American transit, people might ride it more often.

My visit to Hong Kong helped to frame many of the arguments I make in this book, but the thesis of this work really began when I was a graduate student in the Design of Urban Places program at the University of California at Berkeley. It was there that I examined the potential of Las Vegas Boulevard South—more commonly known as "The Strip"—to become a pedestrian friendly, multi-modal transit corridor. At the time, a new transportation system was being planned that would serve the entire length of the Strip, a distance of 3.9 miles. I felt much of the transit proposal was flawed and predicted it would never be the popular attraction that many anticipated. The chosen transit system was an elevated monorail, and its route was *behind* the resorts that line the eastern side of the Strip, offering passengers immediate views of parking lots, garages, and maintenance sheds, too far removed from Las Vegas Boulevard to offer the entertainment passengers would desire. It is really from the ground plane of Las Vegas Boulevard that people experience the Strip, not along tracks a quarter-mile to the east and thirty feet in the air. Using case studies of what many consider to be successful *and* enjoyable transportation systems in the United States, a strong argument was mounted against the monorail and its planned route. Instead, my proposal called for a more pedestrian-scaled, ground-level transit system that allowed passengers a better opportunity to consume the spectacle of this exciting resort community—smack in the middle of the road, immersed in the glitz and the fantasy of Las Vegas Boulevard.

While conducting research for that thesis, I found numerous municipalities that were just beginning to supplement their existing bus routes with other forms of mass transit. Some cities wanted to resurrect historical forms of public transportation, while others were looking to the future of transit technology. Regardless of the approach, environmental concerns, economics, and efficiency were garnering all the attention. The experience offered to the passenger—the "fun factor"—did not weigh anywhere within the transportation proposals. So I began work on this book, to help transit planners, designers, elected officials, enthusiasts, and supporters understand why certain transit systems in America are valued by the public, while others struggle for ridership.

To illustrate these points, I use my own extensive experiences aboard this nation's transit systems. Some will undoubtedly find a certain bias toward particular systems, which can be expected given the title of this book. I strive, however, for objectivity in the analysis, as the findings are not based entirely upon my own reactions but on the observations of other passengers as well. From this empirical research, I offer anecdotal evidence—personal passenger accounts—that give credence to my analyses and arguments. I believe that the reader will find these passenger accounts, those outside of my own, the most illuminating. They were for me.

I end this preface with one such personal account, involving another passenger and me. It was from a simple conversation I had with a fellow straphanger that I realized that public transit can be designed to be more enjoyable and, because it can be a setting for public life, offer inherent social benefits as well. After reading this book, it is my sincerest hope that others will believe in the societal good that public transportation can deliver if designed appropriately. So here is the story:

A pleasant looking man boarded the streetcar near the United Nations Plaza at Jones and Market Street in San Francisco and took a seat behind me. He was interested in my camera, and we were casually talking about digital technology, such as cameras and cell phones with video capability. I showed James (he introduced himself about five minutes into our conversation) how cell phones could now record short movies and then conducted a brief demonstration on the passing

QUIRKY, COLORFUL, AND INTRICATELY DETAILED, HONG KONG'S FLEET OF DOUBLE-DECKER TRAMS
PROVIDE EYE-PLEASING ENJOYMENT FOR PASSENGERS AND PEDESTRIANS ALIKE.

scene outside our window. James recalled how this technology brought the first horrific scenes of the terrorist bombings in London's Underground transit system to the media. Our initial small talk evolved into a more serious conversation, and we began discussing the devastation wrought on New Orleans by Hurricane Katrina. James was retelling a scene he had witnessed on the news about a couple trapped in their car, surrounded by floodwaters with an alligator lurking about, seemingly waiting for them to exit. I could not recall what alligators normally eat (other than the occasional toy poodle), but James educated me on their diet. I had not been keeping up with the latest news on the disaster, but James filled me in, saving me fifty-cents for a newspaper and relaying the news in a more thoughtful, heartfelt manner than most media talking-heads could have.

Our conversation progressed onto a variety of topics, and during our transit ride I learned a lot about James. He was born in Houston but came to California when he was a toddler. He still gets back to Houston at least once a year to visit his extended family, and he said he enjoys the city but is frustrated with the relentless sprawl and the confusing network of highways. I asked James where he was going that day, and he told me Davies Medical Center. Without any further inquiry from me, James then uttered a simple sentence that changed the course of the conversation and gained the interest of all those within earshot: "I'm sick, you see."

James is HIV positive, an illness he contracted when his life revolved around a glass pipe and "dirty women," as he put it. He has been clean for thirty-eight months, and, other than missing two front teeth (a common side-effect of crack abuse), he looked and sounded completely healthy. Yet his regular trips to Davies for his treatments provide a haunting reminder of a life from which he has tried to flee for over three years. James, being a man of little monetary means, rides the streetcar to his medical appointments. While many argue that public transit can improve our quality of life, James relies on public transit merely to prolong his.

Obviously, the chance to meet a recovering crack-addict who is HIV positive is hardly an opportunity transit officials would promote in an effort to boost ridership. Nevertheless, it is a rare opportunity when one can talk so candidly with another who is struggling to overcome an illness and an addiction that has become so pervasive in modern society. It may be difficult for some to comprehend, but our frank discussion was enlightening. Those around us seemed uninterested in the conversation until James was discussing what life is like as a recovering substance abuser with a lethal disease. Passengers previously pretending not to listen didn't even bother to avert their gaze, and we all stared fixedly at James as he told his story with the quiet poignancy of a great orator.

James stood up when the streetcar approached Duboce Avenue. We shook hands, exchanged well-wishes, and I watched as James off-boarded, suddenly concerned for his welfare. I got the sense James was more light-hearted after our conversation. Assumedly, James does not receive the daily social attention he would prefer or deserve. Openly discussing a serious illness or malady can be psychologically therapeutic for those inflicted (something we have witnessed from the elderly, who often like to discuss their physical ailments in great detail). I like to think, simply by lending an ear, that I made a positive difference in James's day. What I did not realize at that moment, however, was the profoundness of our social exchange and the positive difference that short transit ride with James was going to make in this passenger's life.

My Kind of Transit

The arguments are strong in support of public transit: it reduces our reliance on non-renewable fossil fuels, relieves traffic congestion, improves air quality, and helps with our home economics. For most people, it is much cheaper to ride transit than to own and maintain a car, and it is much safer as well. Planners, developers, environmental designers, politicians, and other urban decision-makers have argued for, and have been successful in, providing attractive destinations for transit users. Pedestrian-friendly, mixed-use developments built around clean, safe, and comfortable transit stations give passengers access to a variety of goods and services, as well as employment and housing opportunities. In spite of these benefits, Americans still seem reluctant to ride transit when given the choice.

What advocates of public transportation are loath to admit is that we Americans love our cars (and trucks), even when gas exceeds $4 per gallon (which is low by international standards). Materialism and status aside, we choose a private vehicle over a public one principally because we have more control and freedom within the vehicle's environment. We can play music (and play it very loud), eat, sing, and thump our hands on the steering wheel. If the weather is nice, we can roll down the window, open the sun-roof, or put the top down. If we are cold, we can adjust the heater to meet our exact comfort level, regardless of our attire. Automobiles are not tied to a fixed route or schedule, and they can go anywhere at anytime. Fellow passengers within an automobile provide us with stimulating conversation. These passengers are also free to kick off their shoes, lean their seats back, and even take a nap. Given these obvious passenger comforts, there really is no mystery surrounding our reluctance to embrace public transportation. Quite frankly, the experience of riding in a car is often more rewarding than that of most public transportation systems, and, when given the choice, people— stubborn as we are—choose better experiences over lesser ones.

While much attention has been given to the environmental benefits, economics, and the quality of the destinations served by public transportation, a major problem with transit design today is that little, if any, attention is given to the journey, the *experience* offered within the transit car. If public transportation is to be marketed successfully to the American masses, advocates of transit need to come to a collective realization. That realization is that some rides are simply better than others— meaning more pleasurable, more exciting, more memorable, more enticing. The chance to ride in a '59 Cadillac convertible, for example, can be a much more compelling offer than a ride in a '75 Buick station wagon, regardless of one's purpose or destination. Both, however, offer a more compelling experience than a ride in a typical city bus. But if a similar choice in transportation needed to be made in San Francisco, does the Buick offer a potentially better experience for the passenger than the city's cable car? Does the Cadillac, for that matter? Both the cable car and the Cadillac promise a remarkable ride, albeit for very different reasons, so the choice may not be so obvious. But this hypothetical conundrum illustrates an important point: when public transportation promises a uniquely rewarding experience, the choice between a public vehicle versus a private one becomes a difficult choice indeed.

The premise of this book is the correlation between passenger enrichment and successful American transit. Realistically, public transit cannot compete for the personal freedoms afforded passengers in a private automobile. If transit is to become an attractive alternative to the

TOP: PUBLIC TRANSPORTATION THAT PROMOTES THE AUTOMOBILE IS A DUBIOUS MARKETING STRATEGY FOR ANY TRANSIT AGENCY, AS SEEN HERE IN DAVENPORT, IOWA.
BOTTOM: COMMERCIAL GRAPHICS APPLIED OVER TINTED WINDOWS CREATE CONDITIONS SO DARK IN THE PASSENGER CABIN THAT OVERHEAD LIGHTS REMAIN ON THROUGHOUT THE DAY. THESE GRAPHICS REDUCE NOT ONLY NATURAL LIGHT TRANSMISSION, BUT VISUAL ACUITY AS WELL.

automobile, the ride itself must offer an experience to passengers that they cannot get within the solitude of their cars. Perhaps the greatest asset that transit possesses, one that many do not recognize, is its potential as a setting for public life. Akin to streets, squares, parks, and plazas, transit vehicles are forms of public space—albeit mobile ones. And if today's planners and urban designers are correct in their presumption that the *public realm* is "the most significant amenity . . . the compensation the city offers its customers for forgoing the suburban amenity package,"[1] then public transit has an inherent advantage over the private automobile. After all, "no public life can take place between people in automobiles."[2]

Recognizing the transit vehicle as public space is vital to exploiting the opportunities for passenger enrichment. Once recognized, purveyors of public space must then take a more pro-active role in the design of transit systems as settings for public life. The design approach, therefore, should not be markedly different for transit than for any public space. Like the successful public settings that have lured people from the privacy of their suburban homes and back onto central-city sidewalks, so, too, must transit court people from the privacy of their cars with a similarly rewarding public setting. In his seminal book, *Great Streets*, Allan Jacobs details the rich public life commonly found along well-designed streets. Beyond "permitting people to get from one place to another and to gain access to property," Jacobs contends, streets should "bring people together . . . encourage socialization . . . be physically comfortable and safe. The best streets create and leave strong, lasting, positive impressions; they catch the eyes and the imagination. They are joyful places to be . . . ."[3] It is not unreasonable to expect public transit, often part and parcel of our great streets, to offer such rewards as well.

Currently, many of America's transit systems do not offer these rewarding experiences. The cabin design of some transit vehicles, particularly buses and commuter trains, does not facilitate a particularly enjoyable or memorable experience for the rider. Windows are often small and tinted, dulling the vibrant colors and shutting out the sounds and smells of an active street life. "In the center of a big city," writes Tony Hiss, who is concerned with the restoration of American cities and landscapes, "people who have been used to window-shopping from the bus on the way home from work find that they can't look out the bus windows at night anymore because these now have a dark-green or bronze tint."[4] These dim views are exacerbated by a recent trend to plaster commercial graphics over the entire exterior (including the windows!) of trains and buses, transforming transit into mobile billboards that promote a particular brand of soft drink, cellular phone service, or—perhaps the most perverse—car dealership. A city's decision to allow its public transit vehicles to endorse the private automobile is a dubious marketing decision at best.

As our views out of the cabin become increasingly dim, the views inside become more important. Alas, the interior seldom offers anything worth our gaze. The typical theater-style seating, in which everyone faces toward the front of the cabin, offers the passenger an immediate view of the back of somebody's head. Inappropriate behavior and vandalism can be prevalent with this orientation of seating, especially at the rear of the transit cars, because policing is difficult. Passengers do not make eye contact with one another, as everybody is facing the same direction. The driver, some distance away at the front of the vehicle, is too focused on the road ahead to be involved with what's happening behind. Though generally safe, there is often a *perception* that a breach in security is certainly possible, perhaps imminent, with the design of most transit vehicles. Unable to see out adequately and unable to see within, our personal space is necessarily violated by the close proximity of strangers, and the sound of what could be delinquent behavior behind us is enough to create an anxious atmosphere within the sealed confines of the transit car. It is no wonder that we often feel a great sense of relief upon finally reaching our destination and exiting the cabin.

Anxiety is not typically felt among users in enjoyable public spaces. Upon leaving these spaces, seldom do users experience relief; more likely it is with some reluctance. The transit car is a public realm that is often forgotten by advocates of responsible public space design. If the transit experience is to be rewarding, it should possess the same engaging qualities that are characteristic of our most successful public spaces. Only when transit passengers exit with some reluctance can transit truly compete against the automobile.

It would behoove those engaged in transit design to familiarize themselves with the paradigms that help guide the design of successful public space. Tony Hiss and J. B. Jackson, for example, contend that successful public space heightens our awareness of the sights, sounds, and smells of our surroundings.[5] Spaces that possess these qualities satisfy our innate desire for environmental contact, yielding memorable experiences. William H. Whyte and Clare Cooper Marcus, among others, argue that successful public space allows us to engage passively or actively with others.[6] These spaces satisfy our innate desire for human contact and contribute to gratifying social experiences. It should come as no surprise that the most popular public spaces are often the result of these two ideological paradigms successfully married. The challenge is to apply these sound ideologies of public space design onto transit as well.

An additional benefit of successful public space is the potential for joy and its resultant effect on sociability. When we are enjoying an experience and see others enjoying the same, our inhibitions lessen, and we often share our enthusiasm and even engage in small talk. Pleasant surroundings put us at ease, and we tend to be more sociable when our comfort level is high. The design of the passenger realm within the transit car and the transit route itself can play an important role in our riding experience and how comfortable we feel along such a ride. If designed poorly, transit cars can elevate tension, induce claustrophobia, and increase our anxiety about others. If designed properly, the transit car can have an atmosphere reminiscent of a bustling sidewalk café, in which we feel relaxed, intrigued, and eager to socialize.

Urban designers and planners have long recognized the social opportunities possible within and around transit spaces. Donald Appleyard and Allan B. Jacobs argue in their urban design manifesto that, "as public transit systems have declined, the number of places in American cities where people of different social groups actually meet each other has dwindled."[7] With the understanding that social engagement among a diverse population can be encouraged within transit, it becomes plausible to argue the role transit could play in relieving such stubborn societal problems as social inequity and intolerance. By its very nature, transit breaks through the socio-economic boundaries of neighborhoods, providing access to those with limited means and mobility. Transit cars, being a mobile form of public space, travel from one neighborhood to the next and often gather a great diversity of people along the way. The rich ride along with the poor, the young with the old, the black with the white, and the gay with the straight. As Appleyard and Jacobs further assert, "People of different kinds meet each other directly. The level of communication may be only visual, but that itself is educational and can encourage tolerance."[8]

Undoubtedly, some will argue that visual communication alone is insufficient to encourage tolerance. The period of racial segregation aboard public transportation provides support for such an argument. Not too long ago, well within memory of our parents and grandparents, transit passengers in the South were instructed where to sit based on the color of their skin. Blacks sat in the back of transit cars, whites up front. Although blacks and whites shared the same space of the transit car and even passed one another when boarding and alighting, the atmosphere could hardly be called communal. In fact, the Jim Crow seating arrangement insinuated inequality. When the white section of the transit car filled, black passengers had to give up their seats, often leaving them little choice except to stand or leave the bus. It was the simple yet courageous action of Rosa Parks—refusing to give up her seat to a white passenger in the black section onboard a bus in Montgomery, Alabama—that helped launch the African-American Civil Rights Movement in 1955.* Because of the efforts of Parks and others, the transit car today provides a magnificently diverse and wonderfully integrated form of public space.

Still, social integration may not ensure social interaction. More than visual communication, active conversation is necessary for true sociability between diverse individuals. One might contend, however, that conversation among strangers with different social backgrounds is just not prevalent, even within the myriad public spaces of cities. Neighborhood parks, for example, are laudable forms of public space, primarily because of the recreational and social opportunities in which they foster. Yet even neighborhood parks tend to be somewhat exclusionary in its users. Users of any neighborhood park are principally residents of that neighborhood. Neighborhoods have always been somewhat segregated in terms of income, race, or age. Even within the most integrated and diverse neighborhood parks, people tend to socialize with others of a

---

* There is often confusion as to whether Rosa Parks sat in the black or white section of the Montgomery bus. According to the Website of the U.S. National Archives and Records Administration, she sat in the black section: "On the city buses of Montgomery, Alabama, the front 10 seats were permanently reserved for white passengers . . . . Mrs. Parks was seated in the first row behind those 10 seats. When the bus became crowded, the bus driver instructed Mrs. Parks and the other three passengers seated in that row, all African Americans, to vacate their seats for the white passengers boarding. Eventually, three of the passengers moved, while Mrs. Parks remained seated, arguing that she was not in a seat reserved for whites. Joseph Blake, the driver, believed he had the discretion to move the line separating black and white passengers. The law was actually somewhat murky on that point, but when Mrs. Parks defied his order, he called the police. Officers Day and Mixon came and promptly arrested her."

similar socio-economic status, or at least they make little or no effort to approach people who appear different. Similarly, William H. Whyte states that plazas "are not ideal places for striking up acquaintances, and even on the most sociable of them, there is not much mingling." He observes that, when "strangers are in proximity, the nearest thing to an exchange is what Erving Goffman has called civil inattention."[9]

Perhaps inattention stems from the fact that, within these open spaces, we are still able to maintain our personal space bubble and even defend our territory, so to speak. Within the transit car, however, the sheer closeness of seating necessitates an invasion of personal space. Each passenger will, at some point, sit directly next to and rub shoulders with people they might not ordinarily associate with in a neighborhood park or downtown plaza. In some instances, the seating arrangement within the transit car encourages riders to make eye contact with one another. Many defuse such an intrusion with conversation. It happens on all forms of transit: airplanes, buses, trains, and even casual carpools. This is especially true if that person is a familiar face, like a fellow commuter. Two people, seemingly very different, sharing the same space at the same time, perhaps even disembarking at the same stop, may actually have something in common. This commonality alone is often sufficient to spark small talk. In other words, the closeness of people within transit cars sometimes does lead to casual conversation. Casual conversation with familiar faces can also lead to community acquaintances. Sociability, therefore, has as much potential within the public realm of the transit car as any town square, city street, or neighborhood park and perhaps more so.

For all of these reasons, public transportation can offer keen insight into the effects of well-designed settings on our willingness to socialize with strangers. Slight nods and smiles exchanged by strangers can be more prevalent in this type of public space than even among the most social of streets, plazas, or parks, especially if the transit car offers a positive setting for interaction. Regular contact with different types of people in positive settings can promote understanding, compassion, and tolerance, and transit may be the great social equalizer.

The design of transit can also have a profound effect on our experience of place. Through our physiological senses, we are able to discern a great deal about the environment, and the best forms of transit invite the sights, sounds, and smells of a city into the passenger cabin. Passengers can determine a great deal about the geography, history, development, and culture of a place as well, so long as the design of the transit car and the route offer the opportunity. For example, many forms of public transit were developed in direct response to the topography and unique landscape features of a city. The type of transit employed and its source of locomotion are often a result of the latest technology of the time, and understanding the evolution of technology—what existed when—allows us to recognize better the historical and geographical development of a city. Development patterns along transit routes also provide insight to the urban morphology of our human settlements. Furthermore, the specific design of transit cars can offer a unique quality, a sense of vitality, and an original animated scene within the place it travels. The type of transit, the size of the car, the size of the windows, whether the passenger car is open to the elements, the orientation of seating, and the transit route itself all contribute to how we as passengers experience our environment and each other.

But what specifically makes for enjoyable transit? And how can transit be designed to promote socialization and a better understanding of place? Again, the answers are not far from those necessary for the design of any successful public space. Environments that are safe and comfortable, that offer wonderful views while also stimulating our other senses with sounds and smells, and that allow us to interact with others or passively people-watch are just a few characteristics of popular public spaces that also make for enjoyable, sociable, and environmentally engaging transit experiences. Fortunately, there are good examples of transit in use today that exhibit these experiential qualities. By examining some of the nation's more enjoyable urban transit systems and those not so, and, by understanding the parallels between successful urban open space and transit, public transportation can offer an experience to passengers that they cannot get in their automobiles.

Municipalities across the nation are wrestling with traffic congestion in their downtown centers and historic districts; at the same time, they are trying to attract still more people to them and are turning to locally based public transit systems to provide a solution. Most conventioneers, for example, are arriving at cities not by car but by plane, and they rely on local transit to get them from the airport to their hotel and then again to the convention center, restaurants, and other points of interest. Tourists face the same, if not greater, challenges as conventioneers, since the area they wish to explore within the city is usually more vast. Transportation is a prime concern for many cash-strapped college students who cannot afford to own and operate an automobile. They rely on transit during the day to get them to their classes and throughout the evening for their excursions to movie theaters, cafés, bars, and nightclubs. People who are too old to operate an automobile safely, and those who are too young to do so legally, need transit for their daily errands and to get them to their favorite social gathering spots within the city. As such, many cities are devising, and some are beginning to implement, local transit systems that offer accessibility choices for these people as well as for all others who work and play in the city in which they reside.

This book focuses on city-specific transport systems of a more intimate and localized nature, scaled more closely to the person and operating more comfortably within the neighborhood or district of a city. Large commuter systems that carry huge crowds over great distances within the city and metropolitan region, such as bus fleets and light- and heavy-rail and subway trains, are very efficient and the workhorses of successful mass transit. Categorically, however, these larger systems lack the charm, compulsion, and ingenuity of the smaller, individualized transport systems in America. Although our larger transport systems move more people physically, our smaller systems move more people emotionally. And, although the transit systems profiled in this book are limited to a single district or route of only a few miles in length, they nevertheless reveal positive planning considerations and design details that can be implemented, wholly or in part, to all transportation systems, big and small. It seems our trains and bus fleets can be more than simply "efficient" by taking a few design cues from their smaller, more personable siblings.

Of the many local, commuter-based public transportation systems utilized across the country, what makes these particular systems special? Why, in San Francisco, do people prefer the imported Milan streetcars over the American PCC cars, even though the fare and the route are exactly the same? Why is Seattle's monorail such a big hit for people of all ages, while the Las Vegas monorail leaves much to be desired? The answer, quite simply, is that the transit systems profiled in the succeeding chapters profoundly illustrate the socially rich and environmentally rewarding experiences that are possible in public transportation. More specifically, the chosen transit systems exemplify the best of a type—the apogee of a particular mode of public transportation. They represent what all forms of public transportation should aspire to be. They were chosen for the unique experience they offer passengers and their innate ability to promote social engagement.

Interestingly, those systems that epitomize a particular mode of transit are often the first of their kind. The cable car debuted in San Francisco and remains the only such system in existence today. While many cities employed a cable car system during the late 1800s and early twentieth century, only San Francisco's cable car was compelling enough to spark a resident revolt against city leaders of the time; a revolt to keep the cable cars in operation. The streetcar in New Orleans, with its slow, easy pace, seems to echo the pace of life in the

Deep South. The St. Charles streetcar, the oldest operating system of its kind in the United States, is a top tourist attraction, beloved by visitors and residents alike. Seattle's Monorail, debuting as public transportation in America during the 1962 World's Fair, arguably provides a more enriching passenger experience and a more visceral thrill than the numerous other elevated transit systems still in existence. Santa Barbara's open-air electric shuttle is fondly admired by municipalities nationwide, and some even attempt to imitate this beach town's wonderful ride, only to fall short. And few will argue that any city's fleet of taxis comes close to the unique experience and social opportunity that New York City's cabs offer.

Not all systems profiled in this book possess the unique qualities of those just mentioned. Other systems that are profiled exhibit lofty aspirations, but they fail to foster fond transit memories. Nevertheless, important lessons can be learned from those systems that began with the best intentions, only to have the final experience compromised.

Throughout this book, the big question I aim to answer is: What are the physical, designable qualities of particular transit systems that promote positive transportation experiences? The answers should appeal to anyone interested in improving the quality of life in their city and who considers public transit a means to achieve that goal.

AN ELEVATED VANTAGE POINT ALONG MAIN STREET, U.S.A. (TOP), GIVES PASSENGERS A UNIQUE PER-
SPECTIVE OF THEIR SURROUNDINGS. THIS HIGHER PERSPECTIVE IS THE MOST DESIRED. ONLY
AFTER THE UPPER CABIN OF AN OMNIBUS REACHES CAPACITY DO PASSENGERS, RELUCTANTLY,
BOARD BELOW (BOTTOM).

CHAPTER ONE

Disneyland: The Fundamentals of an Enjoyable Ride

"Disneyland is dedicated to the ideals, the dreams, and the hard facts that have created America . . . with the hope that it will be a source of joy and inspiration to all the world."

"To all who come to this happy place—welcome!"

—WALT DISNEY, JULY 17, 1955[1]

The designers of this world-famous amusement park have never created a ride that is purely functional or utilitarian. Every detail of every element within Disneyland is there for a higher purpose: to enrich the visitor's experience. This is true regardless if the ride is a roller coaster or a simple park transport.

Great cities provide many choices in mobility for exploring their various urban spaces. Disneyland, itself a city of sorts, does so as well. With Main Street, U.S.A., the folks at Disney attempted to capture the best of American urbanity, and transit is an important component that helps to achieve that goal. Transit is an integral, inseparable part of Main Street, a quality that adds unique animation and delight.

Disneyland incorporates a variety of transportation systems along Main Street and beyond. These include scaled-down versions of railroads, park trams, horseless carriages, and riverboats, among others. This chapter will focus on three of the park's transit systems, as these have the greatest relevance to transportation design and planning in our cities today: a past system that is currently extinct in America but deserves resurrection, one that can be readily found in the United States today, and one that many believe represents the future of public mass transit. Respectively, these systems are the omnibus, the street-car, and the monorail.

OMNIBUS

If one studies passengers about to board the omnibus—an open-air, canvas-canopied, double-decker car modeled after the ones used in New York City during the 1920s—behavioral patterns emerge. Most notably, passengers exhibit an unbridled exuberance, regardless of age. When the omnibus approaches, their pace quickens, their steps spring, and giddiness abounds. This by itself is something transit planners should take note of. Considering the competition that the omnibus faces, it is an amazing feat to elicit such excitement from park-goers. Many might conclude that, in the context of Space Mountain, Pirates of the Caribbean, or the Matterhorn, a half-mile ride along Main Street in a slow-moving omnibus would elicit emotions of indifference rather than delight, but the omnibus holds its own. While this form of transportation may have been commonplace along the streets of Manhattan a few generations ago, it looks like nothing on the road today, and crowds gather gleefully for a chance to ride this unusual transit vehicle.

Further observation of boarding passengers yields another inter-esting behavioral pattern: when an omnibus becomes available to board, passengers scramble for a seat on the upper deck; few, if any, prefer the lower level. It is only when the upper-deck reaches capacity that passengers, somewhat reluctantly, begin filing into the seats below. It is curious why people immediately prefer the upper deck. The lower cabin, for instance, has excellent views out, and the plush seats, upholstered in rich, red leather, look inviting and comfortable. The cozy seating lines the perimeter of the lower cabin, allowing people to face one another for easy conversation. These lower seats are also close to the driver, a jovial being who is fun to talk to and who can answer many questions. The lower cabin seems a joyful place to be. Yet passengers, regardless of age, gender, or cultural background, overwhelmingly forego the apparent comfort and convenience of the lower deck and instead race up the steep, narrow staircase with an optimistic hope that they will be rewarded with a better experience up top.

After many trips within the omnibus and careful attention to people's reactions, the reasons people prefer the upper level become evident. The first is the promise of a different perspective. People continuously seek unique experiences, and the ride along Main Street, at a height level with the second story of the passing buildings, provides such a thrill. No other form of transit offers such a vantage point, where passengers are elevated above the hustle of the bustling crowds yet are close enough to the ground as to not induce acrophobia and, more importantly, still be able to hear people's voices, recognize their faces and expressions, take in the scents from the many eateries that line Main Street, and, thus, remain engaged with the street life. But the promise of a unique perspective does not guarantee a relaxing, safe experience. After all, there is no official keeper of the peace on the upper level, and one may assume that, without such an authoritative figure, feelings of insecurity may be prevalent. But the sense on the upper level of the omnibus (and all double-decker buses, it seems, even in the intensely urban areas of London and Hong Kong, for example) is of safety and calm. Tony Hiss, author of *The Experience of Place*, describes this calm as a sense of buoyancy. Hiss argues that, when people feel more in control of their environment, it helps them relax. He even uses Disneyland as an example:

> "This sense of buoyancy is deliberately evoked at Disneyland, where all the buildings are scaled down to something like seven-eighths size. This is not enough of a reduction to make

the buildings look like miniatures, but I've noticed at Disneyland that even this slight shrinkage does have the effect of helping people relax and feel more in control of their circumstances."[2]

Environments can loom over us and make us feel small, or we can loom over our environments, giving us a sense of control and peace of mind. In the case of the omnibus, that elevated vantage point gives us that sense of control—buoyancy—over Main Street. We float above the crowds and our surroundings with a commanding presence and an unobstructed view. It seems people intuitively understand that an elevated position is relaxing and rewarding, thus making the upper cabin the preferred choice of patrons.

The Disneyland omnibus is a proven crowd favorite. Unlike vintage trolleys, which are enjoying renewed popularity in cities small and large throughout the nation, there seems to be reluctance to resurrect the omnibus in America. Though modern-day omnibuses see heavy use as sightseeing vehicles and as public transit in cities all over the world, American cities seem to favor articulated buses. There is not much difference between today's double-decker buses and articulated buses, as both generally seek to double carrying capacity by adding a second passenger cabin. In the case of the articulated bus, that second passenger cabin is attached to the rear of the first, creating a more train-like appearance. The omnibus, instead, places that second passenger cabin up above, maintaining a shorter wheelbase. This may seem like a trivial detail, but the overall effect on both the passenger and pedestrian is far greater with double-deckers. What the double-decker does is accommodate just as many passengers as an articulated bus but with these added benefits: it has a unique form; it offers better visibility from the street, because it looms over other vehicular traffic; it provides a different perspective and, thus, a different experience to passengers above; it maintains a smaller turning radius, thereby eliminating the need to whittle away street corners to facilitate its movement; and it provides two more humanly scaled passenger cabins rather than one long corridor.

In spite of these obvious benefits, double-decker transit vehicles are rare in North America. It seems a shame, as an elevated vantage point is a principal reason why sport utility vehicles (SUVs) became so popular with the motoring public. Omnibuses offer a higher vantage point still, which could effectively draw people away from their cars simply for the unique perspective an elevated cabin offers. In Disneyland, it is safe to assume that the upper cabin is the predominant reason park-goers find the omnibus attractive. A simple detail really—an elevated seat—can transform a mundane transit experience into a memorable one.

STREETCAR

It's difficult to say what transit system is more popular on Main Street, the omnibus or the streetcar. For a passenger, the choice between the two is a tough choice indeed. Popularity is difficult to measure, because the two transit vehicles are rarely, if ever, at the same location boarding at exactly the same time. Otherwise, it would be a worthwhile exercise to watch passenger behavior to determine what system promises the greatest joy and to speculate why. But, as it is, both vehicles routinely fill to capacity. What we *can* measure, empirically, is giddiness: the point where people, regardless of age, get excited and move quickly, with alacrity, almost running to get a seat; where parents abandon their kids for an "everyone for oneself" selfish pleasure; where one can actually discern a change in pitch in one's voice to a higher tone just prior to boarding. This we could measure on a hypothetical "Giddiness Index." If such an index were created, odds are the streetcar might rank slightly higher than the omnibus, meaning that, on a quick observation by a potential passenger, the streetcar promises a slightly more rewarding experience. But this would be splitting hairs, as there are no losers.

So what is it about the streetcar that prompts mature adults to trade composure for silly pleasure? The biggest factor is likely the streetcar's source of locomotion, its literal horsepower. Animals have the ability to move us physically or emotionally. In Disneyland, animals do both. Main Street's most popular public transit is a horse-drawn rail-car, the type that was ubiquitous in America during the mid-1800s. Making its way from Town Square to Sleeping Beauty Castle with an easy, five-mile-per-hour clip-clop pace, pedestrians abandon the side-walks and flock to the streetcar for a better look. Adults smile and point; incredulity is evident on every child's face. No form of transit in the park seems as engaging as this one.

In addition to its animal magnetism, the streetcar is popular with both pedestrians and passengers, because of transparency. There are no walls, doors, or windows to enclose the passenger cabin—just rows of comfortable wooden benches with a fanciful roof overhead, sup-ported by rather inconspicuous square-tube posts. The streetcar is really little more than wooden benches on a wooden platform affixed to steel wheels on steel rails. It is a very simple yet very compelling vehi-cle. The open-air cabin offers passengers the sights, sounds, and smells of Main Street without obstruction. And these passengers glid-ing slowly by, seem to engage pedestrians as well. There is a strong sense of connectedness between passenger and pedestrian, presum-ably because of the lack of physical barriers. Certainly, we are drawn to animals, but we are drawn to people as well.

Despite the wonderful qualities of Disneyland's streetcar, one design detail merits criticism: the streetcars are fitted with running boards to facilitate boarding and alighting and, presumably, to provide a place for standees. This was a common design detail in the urban horse-drawn streetcars of yore, and, when used efficiently, that effec-tively doubled the carrying capacity of the transit car. The running board is an important detail in public transportation, because it offers those who must (or choose to) stand a worthwhile experience, perhaps better than those who are seated. When given the choice to sit or stand, almost without exception passengers choose the former. Those who

TOP: THE RACE IS ON, AS CROWDS CLAMOR TOWARD THE STREETCAR FOR A SEAT.
BOTTOM: THE HORSE-DRAWN STREETCAR PROVOKES UNBRIDLED WONDERMENT AMONG ADULTS
AND KIDS ALIKE, PULLING THEM INTO THE STREET FOR A CLOSER LOOK.

remain on their feet throughout the transit journey are often further penalized, as the cabin's windows are typically located and sized only for those seated, limiting the standee's view. Riding transit can be an arduous and dull experience for those relegated to stand after a long day at work, cut off from the sights and activities of the passing street scene. Running boards, however, provide just compensation for foregoing a seat. They reward standees with completely unobstructed views. They move standees closer to the action, to the hustle and bustle of the street. Riding on a running board provides a visceral thrill, as one must remain focused and strong throughout the ride as the threat of falling into the flow of traffic becomes real. This threat heightens our awareness, sharpens our senses, and offers an exhilarating pleasure that is very different from what those safely seated experience. In this instance, choosing to stand or sit within such a car is not an obvious choice.

The reason the running boards on Disneyland's streetcar deserve criticism is quite simple: the conductor prohibits anyone from standing on them during the ride. The running boards' mere presence is an invitation for use. To have that invitation revoked is disheartening and makes little sense. Pedestrians, for example, are allowed to walk in the middle of Main Street, in front of oncoming transit vehicles. Such an action is presumably more dangerous than standing on the running boards of a slow-moving vehicle. Nevertheless, the running boards remain off-limits to passengers, except for helping one get on or off the car.

Revocation of running board use aside, the streetcar offers a remarkable ride. Arguments will persist over the humaneness of animal power as a source of locomotion. Certainly, the horses comprise much of the draw for passengers and onlookers alike, but the form of the streetcar itself is inviting and would remain so even if powered by steam or electricity. If everything else were held constant—a slow, easy pace, comfortable seating, an open-cabin, fancy and whimsy, and friendly conductors in period attire—the streetcar would still offer a treasured, fun-for-the-entire-family experience.

MONORAIL

The monorail is the only park conveyance that shuns nostalgia. Riverboats, streetcars, omnibuses, horseless carriages, and steam locomotives all reflect civility and technology of a time past. The monorail, though it was introduced to Americans via Disneyland in 1959, still appears to be travel ahead of its time. Its sleek form quietly glides along an elevated, rather delicate superstructure, attracting attention from all those who dream of the future. While the streetcars and omnibuses invite the elder crowd to reminisce, the monorail is a big hit with children, who have little history to reflect upon. Its elevated position gives kids, both literally and metaphorically, a new perspective on the world.

As with every park attraction, a ride on the monorail is more about experience than efficiency. Disneyland's monorail shuttles passengers between just two places in the park: the Downtown Disney district and, quite fittingly, Tomorrowland. Though the distance between these two themed lands is less than a half-mile as the crow flies, the monorail flies a more circuitous two-and-a-half mile course, blending sightseeing with passenger shuttling. The additional distance offers an important lesson in transportation planning: the most direct route may not be the most pleasurable. Passengers do not seem to mind the extra time it takes to get to their destination. On the contrary, they seem to support enthusiastically the detours.

Designed for rapid transit, the monorail trains that Disneyland employs are capable of fairly high speeds, close to seventy miles per hour. Again, the goal for all park rides, even those that are just park transportation, is a joyful experience. It would be difficult to appreciate the scenery in the park, hear the happy crowds below, or feel comfortable entering a turn at seventy miles per hour. The passenger's experience takes precedent above all else. Aware that excessive speed greatly diminishes a passenger's enjoyment, operators pilot the monorail at a more leisurely pace, barely half its potential velocity.

THE DISNEYLAND MONORAIL PROVIDES LESSONS IN INTEGRATION AND ENGAGEMENT. THE TRACKS BRING TRAINS THROUGH THE HEART OF THE THEME PARK AT AN ELEVATION THAT OFFERS UNIQUE VIEWS WHILE MAINTAINING CONNECTEDNESS BETWEEN PASSENGER AND PEDESTRIAN.

Unlike the streetcars and omnibuses, which are confined to a direct route on Main Street, the meandering path the monorail follows guarantees that this transit system is a highly visible and integral component throughout the park. This may be the most important factor as to why it is such an enjoyable mode of park transit, to both passengers and onlookers. The train begins at Downtown Disney, glides past Main Street, then skirts alongside the edge of the park, with the juxtaposition of reality and fantasy in full view. Before reality becomes too overwhelming, the train delves back into the park, encircles the Matterhorn, loops around Fantasyland, and then doubles back to Tomorrowland. From there, the monorail whisks people through the Hollywood Pictures Backlot of the adjoining California Adventure theme park, over a whimsical replica of San Francisco's Golden Gate Bridge, through the Grand Californian hotel, and back to Downtown Disney. Throughout the journey, the monorail tracks bank left and then right, climbing slightly and then falling gently, taking passengers away and then bringing them closer to the experience on the ground. At some places along the route, the passing monorail overhead seems almost low enough to touch. Faces are easily recognized, and delight is apparent in both passengers and pedestrians. In many ways, the monorail feels like a placid roller-coaster, an experience that could not be further from those offered by most transit systems. The monorail is as much an attraction in Disneyland as are the other rides in the park, eliciting broad smiles from big crowds.

The monorail's passenger cabins also play a central role in the experience. More than just providing comfort, the cabins easily allow everyone aboard to gawk at the park amenities below. Numerous clear windows that can slide open during those warm Anaheim days allow the sights and sounds of the boisterous activity in the park to enter the cabin freely. Some seats are better than others, of course; not everyone is guaranteed a window seat. Regardless of where one is seated, though, the views out are still compelling. There is one place that offers the best view, an unparalleled panorama of the park: the nose of the train, with its aerodynamic shape, provides a narrow space for a few lucky passengers to sit with the train operator. The windshield is steeply raked, providing a cockpit-like environment reminiscent of fighter jets. The space is tight, but the views are worth the cramped quarters. What is perhaps most intriguing is that the lucky few actually sit fore of the pilot. In almost every vehicle, be it public transit or private automobile, the driver is given the foremost seat. The best a passenger can be given is the shotgun location. Not so with Disneyland's monorail, where the train operator takes a back seat, allowing passengers to snug up in the conical-shaped space and enjoy an unobstructed view above, out, and below. Subtle details, such as allowing passengers to sit up front to see what the driver sees, elevates an already enjoyable experience to something extraordinary.

LEARNING FROM THE LAND OF MAKE-BELIEVE

Disneyland's omnibuses, streetcars, and monorails exemplify attention to detail that appeal to a passenger's emotions. Sadly, such attention is missing in many American transit systems today. While some may contend that the experience on Main Street is a contrived one, devoid of the serendipity that makes true urban environments special, Main Street is, nonetheless, unique and delivers a universal feeling of delight. The important lesson here is that the park's transit systems were engineered not for the sole purpose of transporting people from one location to the next but for doing so in a way that provides a joyful experience for the passenger, regardless of age, gender, or cultural background.

Disney's designers are keenly aware of the sensual delight that is not only possible, but necessary for successful transportation. To bill itself confidently as the "Happiest Place on Earth," great pains are taken to ensure that every detail in each transit system is not purely functional but contributes in some way to emotional happiness. The physical qualities that are inherent in Disneyland's transportation systems—colorful, unique circulators with an easy pace and a pedestrian-scale, transparency, comfortable seating with a choice in orientation, opportunities for social interaction with fellow passengers or with transit operators, and engaging transit routes, even if a bit circuitous—are fundamental to the park's success. If we could compile the frequency, duration, and intensity of smiles for the transit systems around the world, it is a safe assumption that Disneyland's would top the list. Indeed, the transit systems employed within the park are benchmarks against which all transit systems should be measured.

While Disneyland's transit systems provide an entertaining experience, they are designed, after all, purely for tourists. Would these transit systems offer similar experiences within real urban settings? Would they appeal both to visitors and residents alike? Are they even practical outside the "Land of Make-Believe"? In short, the answer is yes, but urban counterparts to amusement park rides take many forms, some similar to Disneyland's and others quite different. It is worth an exploration of this nation's most unique transit systems and the resultant joy they offer both to passengers and onlookers. This is the objective of the succeeding chapters. Let us begin our journey.

TOP: ON THE APPARENT EDGE OF THE WORLD, SPECTACULAR VIEWS OF SAN FRANCISCO AND
PULSE-QUICKENING THRILLS CAN BE HAD ABOARD THE CABLE CAR.
BOTTOM: A FAMILY BOARDS THE CABLE CAR IN THE MIDDLE OF CALIFORNIA STREET IN CHINATOWN.
THE SEEMINGLY PERILOUS CONDITIONS ARE ACTUALLY QUITE SAFE.

CHAPTER TWO

Cable Cars in San Francisco

"Of course, the best way to catch a city while it's living is to sneak up on it. Walking is ideal but not always practical on San Francisco's hills, so the most logical substitute is a slow-moving, quiet, open vehicle—precisely the features of a cable car."

—CHRISTOPHER SWAN, *CABLE CAR*[1]

Native to San Francisco, the cable car is a simple response to the city's undulating landscape. Prior to its introduction, public transportation within the city consisted predominantly of horse-drawn streetcars, carriages, and omnibuses. Yet the grades along San Francisco's streets often proved too steep for the animals, a problem that was exacerbated by the foggy climate of the region. Horse hooves unable to get a toehold on damp cobblestones was a regular sight, occasionally leading to catastrophe. Broken legs were not uncommon when horses attempted to pull loaded cars on wet pavement up a steep incline. And such an injury meant the cruelest form of workers' compensation: euthanasia.

Andrew Hallidie, a Scottish mining engineer and son of an inventor of wire-rope cable, witnessed such a macabre event. In an 1871 report to the Mechanics' Institute, Hallidie recalled "seeing the difficulty and pain the horses experienced in hauling the cars up Jackson Street, from Kearny to Stockton Street, on which street four or five horses were needed for the purpose—the driving being accompanied by the free use of the whip and voice, and occasionally by the horses falling and being dragged down the hill on their sides, by the car loaded with passengers sliding on its track."[2] That incident motivated the young Hallidie to begin a quest to provide a better, more humane method of transporting passengers up and over San Francisco's treacherous hills. Only a few years later, in the fittingly foggy predawn morning of August 1, 1873, and on a precipitous slope along Clay Street near the top of Nob Hill, Andrew Hallidie and a team of workers—all human—introduced a unique form of street transportation to the world.

The cable car technology that San Francisco spawned soon migrated to Oakland and to other cities throughout the world. Chicago, Edinburgh, London, Los Angeles, New York, Seattle, and Sydney were a few of the world's great cities that implemented cable car systems of their own. The cable car's heyday was short-lived, however. In 1888, technology was perfected for the electric streetcar, providing a more efficient and cost-effective carrier of people. Still, many preferred the simplified beauty of cable car technology. The tangle of overhead wires that fed power to the streetcars, though far more economical than underground cables, was pleasantly absent from the design of the subsurface system of the cable car. The invisibility of the cable car's source of locomotion made for a more elegant street scene and created an amazing animation of intricately detailed cars gliding effortlessly on rails through the streets of San Francisco.

If the electric streetcar were its only competition, the cable car would undoubtedly be more prevalent today. Other events accelerated the demise of the cable car. The devastating earthquake of 1906 demolished much of the underground infrastructure of San Francisco's cable cars in a matter of seconds. The system was repaired over the years but never to the extent of the pre-earthquake routes. Then, in the 1930s, diesel buses proved they were just as capable of transporting passengers over the steep inclines as the beloved cable cars. By the

1940s, buses were the preferred transit alternative by those in power in the city. The only problem, however, was eloquently summed up by Friedel Klussman, a citizen-activist driven by her devotion to the cable cars and known for her public crusades to save them. Klussman publicly pondered, "How can you fall in love with a bus?"[3]

Her vocal sentiment, though touching and instrumental in preserving some of San Francisco's cable cars, went unheard in other parts of the world where this form of public transit was employed. City by city, the cable cars fell victim to diesel bus technology. In 1960, the city of Dunedin, New Zealand, the only other city at the time to utilize cable cars as public transport, shut down its system. After nearly a century-long global presence, the cable car became, yet again, unique to San Francisco.

It is unlikely one can fall in love with a bus, as Ms. Klussman insinuated, but can one actually be smitten with *any* mode of public transportation, particularly an American one? If that mode is San Francisco's cable car, then the answer is a resounding "yes!" Throughout their existence, San Francisco's cable cars have touched the lives of residents and visitors alike. They have been the subjects of paintings, poems, and photographs and the setting for many a wedding ceremony. Merchants have been astute in marketing the heart-fluttering appeal of these transit cars to help promote their own business. A quick look in the local phone book turns up a dizzying number of establishments that have incorporated "cable car" into their name: bail bondsmen, clothiers, coffee shops, dentists, dry cleaners, jewelers, opticians, photographers, and pizza parlors, to name some.

San Francisco's cable cars are frequently mentioned in song and literature as well. The cable car is the only human creation mentioned in the homesick soliloquy, "I Left My Heart in San Francisco," made famous by singer Tony Bennett. Rudyard Kipling found the technology that allowed the cars to "run up and down a slit in the ground for many miles" miraculous, and he noted with further incredulity that "the Cable-Cars have for all practical purposes made San Francisco a dead level. They take no count of rise or fall, but slide equally on their appointed courses from one end to the other of a six-mile street. They turn corners almost at right angles; cross other lines, and, for aught I know, may run up the sides of houses."[4] Herb Caen, the famous and much admired local newspaper columnist, authored a children's book featuring Charlie, a personified cable car, as the protagonist. In the story, Caen likens the ride aboard the cable car to a roller coaster and concludes, "it's about the best ride in the world."[5] Indeed, the cable car is such a beloved bit of machinery that, in 1964, Stewart Udall, then Secretary of the Interior, declared it a National Historic Landmark. It is almost inconceivable that such a profound declaration is warranted for public transit, but the cable car is that special. The iconography of San Francisco's cable car is unparalleled. For many who have experienced the ride, the cable car *is* San Francisco, a product of its landscape and a beloved historical treasure.

The cable car is, arguably, the epitome of enjoyable urban transportation. People line up at the Powell Street turn-around hundreds deep and often wait for an hour or more for a ride on this famous San Francisco landmark. The cable car, a means to a destination, is certainly a destination in itself. No visit to San Francisco is complete without climbing aboard this wonderful form of public transit.

The cable car's appeal is due to the experience it offers its passengers, and it begins with boarding. Along the cable car route, one will not find any transit stations, the purpose of which is often for people to purchase tickets and wait for the circulators. For the cable car passengers, sidewalks take the place of transit platforms, and cable car conductors take the place of ticket-dispensing machines and turnstiles.

Passengers may choose to board at one of the terminal stops of each route, where they witness the archaic but enthralling ceremony of turning the cable car on a rotating wooden platform in preparation for its journey in the opposite direction. Some, however, opt to hop aboard from one of the many stops along the cable car route. These stops are simple

THE INTERSECTION OF CALIFORNIA AND POWELL STREETS. OTHER THINGS BEING EQUAL, WHICH TRANSIT VEHICLE WOULD YOU RATHER RIDE?

and nondescript—small signs affixed to metal posts at the edge of the sidewalk, similar to a common bus stop. In Chinatown, the signs are written both in English and Chinese, but otherwise the stops are nothing extraordinary. What is extraordinary, however, is the procedure one must undergo to board the cable car at one of these intermediate stops. While buses are able to pull over to the sidewalk's edge to facilitate boarding, the cable car is affixed to rails in the middle of the street, a path from which it cannot stray. Intersections along the steep hills of San Francisco are graded level, and, thus, the middle of these intersections is the easiest location for cable cars to stop to allow passengers to board and alight. The middle of an intersection is a place pedestrians rarely occupy and for good reason: it is typically a dangerous zone. But, with the cable car stopping traffic in all directions, the intersection is almost entirely safe for pedestrians. Nevertheless, when one steps off the curb and walks into a realm typically inhabited only by automobiles, a visceral thrill becomes evident, one that is heightened with the hint of danger. Heart rates elevate, adrenaline flows, and anticipation builds. An exciting transit journey has begun.

Once aboard, the sights, sounds, and smells of San Francisco are offered without restriction to the cable car riders, due to the open-air design of the end cabins. Wooden seating, similar to comfortable park benches, face outward from the end cabins, giving riders magnificent and unobstructed views of the city. The vehicle's modest speed, only 9.5 miles per hour, also facilitates sightseeing and people-watching. The view is as pleasing to pedestrians as well. One never tires of walking along the sidewalks of San Francisco and seeing a cable car packed with smiling faces slip slowly by.

Perhaps the most intriguing design detail is the running board found along the sides of the end cabins. These running boards facilitate boarding and alighting by acting as an intermediate step between the street and the elevated cabin. Most interesting, these running boards offer an attractive alternative to the inviting bench seats. Indeed, one often hopes that all available seats are taken, leaving the passenger with standing as the only option. Chivalry is alive and well on the cable car, as passengers are quick to offer up their seats for a better position on the running boards. ("Here, Ma'am, take my seat. No, I insist!") The standing passengers, relying on their own balance and strength to keep from falling into passing traffic, are rewarded with an exhilarating ride through the streets of San Francisco. People hanging off the sides of the cable car, grinning from ear-to-ear and some even waving to onlookers along the sidewalk, is testament to the unique and delightful experience that is possible in urban transit.

The cable car fancifully announces its arrival, not with a horn or a computerized voice (a recent trend in bus design) but with the ringing of a bell. What makes this bell special is that it is rung by human hands, meaning the ensemble of "ding-a-ding-DINGS" is as individual as the cable car conductors themselves. Each operator's repertoire of "dings" has become something special for the city's residents and visitors, whether one rides the cable or not. Every year, using Union Square as the venue, the city holds a bell-ringing event, a public concert, if you will, showcasing the musical talent of the cable car's conductors. The event is a crowd-pleaser among residents and visitors alike, a special gathering to celebrate this beloved urban amenity.

In addition to the cabin's design details, the cable car routes—the street scenes, hilltops and the views beyond—provide memorable experiences. Consider for a moment one of the three routes: the Powell-Hyde line. The journey begins on a wooden turntable at the intersection of Powell and Market streets, the historical nexus of down-town San Francisco. Along this line, the cable car passes such city gems as Union Square and its famed shopping district and the St. Francis and Sir Francis Drake hotels. Famous restaurants, bars, and boutiques, all bustling with people, are passed along the way. The car continues its ascent up Nob Hill, along the edge of Chinatown. From the summit, passengers are rewarded with views down California

Street to the financial district, the Bay Bridge, and the California Street cable car line. As the car makes its way down the north face of Nob Hill and winds its way to Russian Hill, quiet neighborhood blocks lined with Victorian-era residences come into view. Near the top of Russian Hill, the cable car pauses at the intersection of Hyde and Lombard streets, the commencement of the "crookedest street in the world." Immediately after this point, an awe-inspiring panorama unfolds: the cable car seemingly plummets down Russian Hill, with fantastic views of San Francisco Bay, Alcatraz Island, Angel Island, and the neighboring hills of Marin County. Just a few short minutes after the journey began, with views of the Golden Gate Bridge now commanding the passenger's attention, the cable car reaches its destination, coming to rest at Aquatic Park, near Ghirardelli Square, the Cannery, and Fisherman's Wharf. In short, many of San Francisco's finest attractions are served along this two-mile cable car route.

The cable car also provides another unique form of passenger enrichment by encouraging social engagement. Indeed, the operation of the cable car practically requires verbal exchange. Unlike many transit systems in operation today, there is no cable to pull or button to press to signal the driver of a "Stop Requested." The passenger must ask one of the two cable car operators, "Can you let me off at the next corner?" These two operators, the grip and the conductor, also converse with each other. The conductor can be found mingling among the passengers, directing them where to sit or stand, cautioning standees of opposing traffic, and announcing transit stops. The conductor also collects transit fare from the passengers. Impersonal metal boxes that take your money when boarding are neither needed nor desired aboard the cable car. Sometime after the cable car pulls away from a stop, the conductor asks, "Does anybody need a ticket?" Passengers respond and pay their fare.

These brief but frequent interactions between operator and passenger initiate a conversation-friendly atmosphere. Tourists feel comfortable asking questions regarding the sights of San Francisco, and the cable car operators are eager to respond. Locals who use the cable car for commuting are often on a first-name basis with the operators. Unlike the notices posted in buses all over the country, commanding, "Do not talk to the driver," conversation is encouraged in the cable car.

While the cable car is usually lively and crowded with tourists in the afternoon and evening, the early morning commute offers a quietly distinct experience. The commuting regulars, sipping their morning tea or coffee, often discuss politics and daily events with each other and the cable car operators. This type of casual conversation seems befitting, as the design and detailing of the cable car's cabin is reminiscent of an inviting urban café. And, like the popular cafés that nurture social relationships, it is common for commuters and operators to develop casual acquaintances with each other within the comfortable confines of the cable car.

Linda's story is a case in point, attesting to some of the benefits of such acquaintances. She lives near the top of Nob Hill, a half-block away from the Powell-Hyde line, and works near Union Square in downtown. Linda is one of the fortunate residents of San Francisco who rely on the cable car as their primary mode of public transportation. In the still quiet of morning, she can hear the bell of an approaching cable car from her apartment, and the "ding-ding-a-ding-DING" offers a cheery substitute for an alarm clock.

Like all the regular commuters on the cable car lines, Linda knows the conductors and grips by name, and the conductors know hers. Every morning before work, she walks to the corner coffee shop to get her cup of pick-me-up before boarding her car to downtown. On occasion, when Linda is running a minute or two behind schedule, the grip will stop the cable car and wait for her. Linda races out to the car, boards, and good morning pleasantries are exchanged. Quiet conversation ensues, usually regarding current events, such as the mayoral race, the performance of the San Francisco Giants or 49ers the day before, or whether the redesign of Union Square is actually appropriate for the city. These conversations often involve fellow commuters as well, and an occasional friendship develops that carries outside the common ground of the cable car.

Linda recalls one particular day when the weather shift was quick. The morning was clear and warm, offering the promise of a pleasant day. By four-o'clock, however, San Francisco's famous fog rolled in, covering downtown in a chilly, damp blanket. Linda, usually aware of this typical pattern, forgot her coat that day. After boarding the cable car downtown, Louis, the car's conductor, offered Linda his special issue S.F. MUNI Cable Car jacket for the ride and walk home. Both knew they would see each other the next day when Linda could return the jacket, and she graciously accepted his favor. There may have been an ulterior motive on Louis's part, as he had somewhat of a fancy for Linda. Nevertheless, the gesture was kind, one that was initiated because of a trusting friendship that developed between operator and passenger on a wonderfully sociable form of public transit.

Linda's cable car experiences are not uncommon. What is uncommon is that a real sense of community can be found within public transit. Great public spaces nurture community by facilitating social engagement. The cable car's design provides such an opportunity and, in many respects, functions like a neighborhood park or town square. Like Linda, countless others will contend that the atmosphere found within San Francisco's cable car is one of the friendliest in the nation. It has to be. When you are seated in the car, shoulder-to-shoulder with tourists snapping pictures, while another passenger is standing on the running board with his legs between your knees, all you can do is quietly laugh to yourself and muse over the realization that, perhaps, Herb Caen was right: the San Francisco cable car is "about the best ride in the world."

CHAPTER THREE

Streetcars in New Orleans and San Francisco

"*STELLA: But there are things that happen between a man
and a woman in the dark—that sort of make everything else seem—
unimportant.*

*BLANCHE: What you are talking about is brutal desire—just—
Desire!—the name of that rattle-trap street-car that bangs through
the Quarter, up one old narrow street and down another . . .*

STELLA: Haven't you ever ridden on that street-car?"

—TENNESSEE WILLIAMS, *A STREETCAR NAMED DESIRE*[1]

Streetcars dominated public transit in America from the late 1880s through the end of World War II. Almost every city and town in the nation had a streetcar line, and such presence signaled prosperity, for streetcars accelerated the growth and expansion of the city. While the automobile has driven the street pattern and urban form of our post-World War II suburban and newer exurban settlements, the streetcar first made the suburb possible. Streetcars, with a leisurely pace, seldom exceeding ten miles per hour, required a compact urban form, with a grid of streets that were accessible and friendly for the pedestrian. The type of growth fed by the streetcar was more healthful and more measured, compared to the Automobile Age. Automobile-fed growth occurred in rapid, almost tumor-like spurts, spreading suburbs great distances from a city's center. For a nation bent on growth after the war, the battle at home between streetcars and automobiles would prove to be a bitter one.

Streetcars vanished from the American landscape shortly after World War II, quickly succumbing to buses and the private automobile. Steel wheels were thought to be Iron Age technology, and rubber "balloon-tires" hinted at a softer, smoother ride. Asphalt roads were being built for cities all over the country during the mid-century and at a much cheaper and faster rate than rails. Diesel engines freed the bus from the net of wires that ensnared the electric streetcar. Though electricity is now considered a more eco-friendly source of locomotion, environmental concerns were hardly on people's minds during the rapid disappearance of our nation's streetcars. Vehicles that could not stray from a fixed track or wires overhead meant less maneuverability and, thus, less freedom. It was, perhaps, this promise of freedom—the ability to travel without constraint—that rang true with the democratic ideals of this country, winning over the American masses. For more than a half-century, Americans have embraced this perception of transportation freedom and the Petroleum Age that gave us vehicles with rubber tires traveling on asphalt roads while burning, until recently, cheap gasoline.

Bruised and battered, the electric steel relics of the past are mounting a comeback. Society today *is* concerned with the rapid consumption of nonrenewable fossil fuels, and electric-powered cars help quench our thirst for oil. Steel wheels on steel rails actually yield a smoother ride than rubber tires on asphalt roads. In cities throughout the nation, buses cannot compete with automobiles, their fossil-fuel consuming cousins, but streetcars can.

As award-winning journalist and urban development critic Roberta Gratz notes, streetcars "are bringing people back to centers, increasing pedestrian activity and street life, bringing people to a downtown to which they don't think they have reason to go, keeping people downtown longer by making it easy to go from place to place, and introducing a car-born and car-bound generation to mass transit in a novel way."[2] Returning after a fifty-year hiatus, streetcars are en route to becoming in vogue, providing a delightful, economically viable form of urban transportation for cities across the nation. Portland, Oregon, is said to have built the first major modern streetcar system in America in 2001. Cincinnati, Ohio, is investing at least $132 million in a new streetcar system, and Columbus, Ohio, is pursuing its own $103 million network of streetcars. Furthermore, as Bob Driehaus reports, "At least 40 other cities are exploring streetcar plans to spur economic development, ease traffic congestion and draw young professionals and empty-nest baby boomers back from the suburbs. . . . Since Portland announced plans for the system," Driehaus continues, "more than 10,000 residential units have been built and $3.5 billion has been invested in property within two blocks of the line . . ."[3] And Charlotte, Little Rock, Kenosha (Wisconsin), Memphis, and Tampa are among those cities that have recently augmented their public transit systems, boosted tourism, and aided revitalization efforts with vintage streetcars.

Though many wonderful streetcar systems (both vintage and contemporary) are in operation today, New Orleans and San Francisco are the focus of this chapter for many reasons. One is their value to commuters. Though the streetcars in these two cities are top tourist attractions, these systems operate beyond a single district, connecting neighborhoods with the workplace, schools, and social gathering spots, thus providing an attractive transit option for residents as well.

Secondly, New Orleans and San Francisco arguably possess the most notable streetcar examples in America. New Orleans is famous for its St. Charles line, surviving two world wars and the worst natural disaster in our nation's history, Hurricane Katrina in 2005. Enmeshed in the culture and folklore of New Orleans, the St. Charles line evokes the leisure, civility, and resilience of the city. San Francisco is special, because it employs streetcars from all over the world. Australia, Belgium, England, Italy, Portugal, and the United States are just a few

TOP: MAHOGANY BENCHES WITH BRASS TRIM, FABRIC SHADES, UNTINTED OPERABLE WINDOWS, AND NAKED INCANDESCENT BULBS ARE JUST A FEW UNIQUE DETAILS FOUND INSIDE THE ST. CHARLES STREETCAR IN NEW ORLEANS.

BOTTOM: EASING ITS WAY THROUGH THE GRASSY "NEUTRAL GROUND" IN THE MIDDLE OF THE STREET, THE ST. CHARLES STREETCAR REQUIRES MOTORISTS TO ADOPT A LEISURELY PACE.

countries represented in San Francisco's fleet. This diversity of quirky machines provides color to the streets of the White City, delighting tourists and residents alike.

More importantly, the diversity of people found within the street-cars of New Orleans and San Francisco makes these urban transport systems truly special. These cities' streetcars connect residents with tourists, the down-and-out with the affluent, white with black, and students with "suits." The French Quarter and the Castro, two of the gay-friendliest neighborhoods in the country, are well served by their respective streetcar lines. By virtue of the neighborhoods through which they travel, these streetcars connect all kinds of people to all kinds of places in a delightfully engaging way. One can't help but wonder if these transit systems reinforce the "live-and-let-live" attitude that is so pleasantly entwined within the culture of these two communities.

NEW ORLEANS

Few transportation systems in the world reflect the context and culture of their city as do New Orleans's streetcars. Seemingly as old as the city itself, olive-green cars ease their way through oak-lined streets. The cabins' antiquated, wood-frame construction echoes the wood-framed antebellum structures that give the city its architectural charm. Their leisurely pace matches the ease with which citizens move about the city. In some ways, these public vehicles exhibit a certain civility and gentility indicative of life in the Big Easy.

The St. Charles streetcar was the oldest continuously operated rail line in the nation; that is, until the summer of 2005. Beginning with horse-drawn cars in 1835, the rails along St. Charles Avenue have seen the evolution from steam power to animal power and finally to electric power in 1893. Unlike other American cities, New Orleans eschewed gasoline power for this transit route, relying on electrically powered streetcars for more than a century. Then on August 29, 2005, the streetcars vanished. Hurricane Katrina's punishing category 3 winds downed the electric poles and overhead wires that fed electricity to the city's streetcars. Though the damage was extensive, transportation officials believed they had dodged a bullet. Breached levees soon proved otherwise. The massive flooding that inundated the city guaranteed that streetcar service would not be restored for many months. With an irony that parallels the fate of this nation's streetcar systems during the mid-twentieth century, buses took over the duties of shuttling passengers along the historic St. Charles rail route. It seemed incongruent that, after a century-and-a-half of continuous operation, anything but a streetcar should pass through St. Charles Avenue.

Thankfully, the bus substitution along St. Charles Avenue was temporary, lasting little more than a few years. But, during that period of inoperability, the historic cars of the St. Charles line proved they were truly the great survivors of our time. In addition to the downed power lines that propelled the city's streetcars, water flooded all twenty-four of the newly built Canal streetcars and six of the seven Riverfront cars, two recently reincarnated lines that serve the city in addition to the historic St. Charles line. Miraculously, all of the historic St. Charles streetcars survived. In December 2006, sixteen months after Hurricane Katrina paralyzed the three streetcar lines in the city, the New Orleans Regional Transit Authority reinstituted limited streetcar service. The famed St. Charles streetcars came to the rescue, providing service for both the Canal and Riverfront routes, in addition to its own limited central business district route. It wasn't until June 22, 2008, that the St. Charles line was fully restored and the welcome sound of the clanking green streetcars rolled down St. Charles Avenue again, in hopes of another hundred years of continuous service.

The street through which the St. Charles streetcar travels—the physical space between the sidewalks—sets this form of urban transport apart from other surface-street systems. Unlike cable cars, shuttles, taxis, and buses that share space with automobiles, St. Charles Avenue supplies the streetcar with its own travel lane. This "neutral ground" (as it is known in New Orleans) is really nothing more than a grassy median through which steel rails and electrical poles provide the infrastructure necessary to propel the streetcar. But this space provides additional greenery to St. Charles Avenue, helping to give the street its characteristic lushness. One increasingly finds joggers running alongside the streetcar tracks, beating paths through the grass of the neutral ground. Located in the middle of the street, this otherwise simply detailed neutral ground is significant. The awaiting passengers, joggers, and streetcars that inhabit the neutral ground set the leisurely pace along St. Charles Avenue. It is a comforting sight, knowing that the median is not only a safe space, but a highly visible one that alerts motorists to the civil nature of the street.

The civility of the street is an apt reflection of the civility aboard the streetcar. The interior of the passenger compartment is rich with detail: polished mahogany seats, wood paneling, plank floors, and brass trim. Large, operable, and untinted windows allow natural light to suffuse the cabin, while passengers who desire relief from glare can simply pull down the fabric shades. Nighttime lighting seems a bit incongruent at first, accomplished with nothing more than naked incandescent bulbs, the type that Blanche DuBois could not stand "any more than a rude remark or a vulgar action."[4] No such civil disobedience is illuminated within these streetcars, however. More accurately, the warm incandescent light reveals a bayou-like simplicity and gentility.

An ingenious detail is found on the wooden bench seats in the streetcar. Reversible backrests allow passengers to face toward the direction of the traveling streetcar or with their back to it. Innately, we prefer to face forward in a moving vehicle, but, when a group of three or four acquaintances boards, this simple detail accommodates their desire to sit and face one another, allowing their conversation to continue. What is most interesting is that such a detail in the transit car is unique. A simple matter—allowing the passenger a modicum of control over the orientation of the seat (something William Whyte deemed so essential for good public space) — is completely absent from transit systems in the United States.[5] The closest thing is a backrest that reclines slightly, found on planes and some trains, but this does nothing to facilitate conversation or views. It is as if the seating in public transportation today takes design cues from popular fast-food restaurants: molded plastic seats that are permanently affixed to the floor offer an uncomfortable rigidity that is essential for a high frequency of occupant turnover. The wooden seats aboard the St. Charles streetcar seem to encourage the passenger to lounge and stay awhile.

Singular details aside, what is most memorable about the ride aboard the historic St. Charles streetcars is the urban context through which they travel. The passing scene is one of quaintness and charm, a civilized urban pattern with a mix of uses, created with leisure and comfort for the pedestrian in mind. The streetcar was part and parcel of these neighborhoods, their raison d'être. Roberta Gratz describes the inseparable nature of transit and neighborhood development through an excellent account of being aboard the St. Charles streetcar:

> "One need only visit the Garden District of New Orleans today to sense the hallmarks of the everyday neighborhoods of the streetcar era. The St. Charles line is the world's oldest continuously operated street railway with regular service provided by an aging but well-maintained fleet of cars much celebrated in photographs and song. Tourists ride it for novelty. Residents ride it for convenience.
>
> "The refurbished 1920s cars, "durable as tanks," offer the incomparable comfort of operable windows and wooden slatted seats that are reversible, so that a group or family of four can face each other for the ride. Live oaks grace the sidewalks. Lushly landscaped antebellum single- and two-family homes tied graciously into the street are interspersed with institutions,

short patches of local commercial services, restaurants, corner stores. New buildings are pedestrian-accessible, fashioned in the street form of the earlier era. Loyola and Tulane universities appear comfortably integrated. Small hotels and garden apartments coexist. The variety is rich but the overwhelming feeling is of a residential, comfortably scaled quarter . . ."[6]

After talking with others about their experiences aboard the St. Charles streetcar, patterns of memorability become evident. These passenger accounts do not differ greatly from Gratz's; in fact, they are remarkably similar. The streetcar's longevity, the reversible mahogany bench seats and the sociability they foster, the operable windows that engage our senses of touch and hearing while allowing better views of the passing landscape, the mature trees and lushness of the street, the grandeur and charm of the Garden District, and the dignity of the universities are just a few characteristics of the St. Charles line that consistently leave fond and lasting impressions in our minds, regardless of who we are and where we come from. These consistent features of wonderment aboard the St. Charles streetcar—history, connection to the urban context, stimulation of the senses, and sociability through architectural detail—offer important lessons about providing a memorable transportation experience. Transit designers would do well to focus upon them.

SAN FRANCISCO

Historically, San Francisco had not exhibited the fondness for streetcar technology that other cities had. In the late nineteenth century, when streetcars were becoming the transit of choice in urban areas throughout the world, San Francisco remained faithful to its beloved cable car system. But the devastating 1906 earthquake, which destroyed much of the city and its cable car infrastructure, shook the fidelity of the cable car public, and streetcars became the foundation of mass transit within San

Francisco. By 1920, Market Street was fitted with four sets of tracks, making it one of the busiest streetcar arterials in the nation. This all changed rapidly once diesel bus technology was heavily touted following World War II, and San Francisco's streetcars, like those in cities across the nation, were fast headed toward extinction. Disappearing for almost fifty years, it wasn't until the close of the twentieth century that San Franciscans witnessed the streetcar's resurgence.

San Francisco's historic cable cars are known the world over, but few people are familiar with the city's vintage streetcar system. While the cable cars ease passenger transport up and over the precipices of San Francisco, the streetcars shuttle people along the flatter terrain of Market Street and the Embarcadero. What is particularly unique about San Francisco's streetcar system is that the fleet is not comprised of only one model of streetcar but rather an assorted collection from cities all over the world. Along the same route, for the exact same fare, transit passengers are afforded different experiences depending upon the vintage streetcar they board. "Part of the attractiveness," notes Rick Laubscher, the president of Market Street Railway, the nonprofit preservation partner of San Francisco's Municipal Railway, is not knowing "what might come along next: a bouncy single-truck streetcar from Portugal; a smooth-riding tram from Australia; a Muni original from the 1910s; even an open-topped boat tram from Blackpool, England, complete with a skull and crossbones flag on the trolley rope" brings whimsy to the transit experience.[7] This promise of variety breaks the transit routine, stirs excitement among riders, and converts even the most devout automobile commuters into strap-hanging believers.

San Francisco's diverse fleet of streetcars provides an excellent opportunity to compare different designs for transit vehicles and their resultant effect on a passenger's enrichment. The route, fare, operation, and relative size remain constant. The only variables are the overall style and decor—the design details—of each streetcar. Two models in particular, sufficiently different from each other, transport the bulk of streetcar passengers along Market Street and the Embarcadero and, thus, deserve an in-depth comparison.

AMERICAN PCC STREETCARS

To combat the growing threat from buses and the private automobile, San Francisco—as well as cities across North America—implemented a redesigned streetcar during the 1930s. Reeling from the growing sentiment that the streetcar was fast becoming outmoded, a committee representing various electric street railway companies was formed in 1929. This committee was tasked with updating the electric streetcar to compete better against its gasoline-powered counterparts. The resulting design, known as the Presidents' Conference Committee (PCC) streetcar, was lighter and quieter and accelerated more smoothly than its predecessors. But it had to be more: if the PCC was to prove that streetcars were not antiquated, it had to have a sleek, contemporary design reminiscent of the time, not one that recalled the turn-of-the-century. Function aside, the most notable quality of the new PCC car was its Art Deco, streamlined exterior. The redesign was handsome and dignified—a triumph considering it was designed by a committee. These "Streamliners," as they were affectionately called, seemed poised to propel streetcar technology well into the twentieth century.

Streamliners, though initially popular in San Francisco and other cities across the continent, eventually lost out to the bus shortly after World War II. Though many claim the demise of the streetcar was the result of the infamous General Motors-led conspiracy, the design of the PCC itself may have contributed to its disfavor.[8] The PCC's streamlined design, though more modern looking than that of earlier streetcars, was strikingly similar to the design of buses of the same era, with one difference: buses did not have the constrictions of a fixed track and overhead wires. Not being tethered to electrical lines or bound to steel rails, buses had greater maneuverability, were cheaper to implement, and, thus, made greater sense.[9] Once onboard the PCC streetcar, the

TOP: THE STREAMLINED, BRIGHTLY-PAINTED AMERICAN "PCC" STREETCARS, SUCH AS THIS ONE
DRESSED OUT IN A BOSTON LIVERY, ADD ROVING SPLASHES OF COLOR ALONG MARKET STREET,
IN SAN FRANCISCO.
BOTTOM: QUIRKY AND FUN, THE TRAMS FROM MILAN, ITALY, BRING SMILES TO ALL THOSE WHO RIDE
THEM . . . EVEN THEIR OPERATORS.

layout and utilitarian decor of the passenger cabin was also similar to buses of the time. One has to wonder: if the PCC had nothing unique to offer passengers of the time, why would people *not* favor the bus over the streetcar?

Today, Streamliners do offer something unique to passengers. These streetcars are attractive largely because of contrast: contrast in style, locomotion, detail, color, and, perhaps most importantly, time. Though commonplace a few generations ago, the streetcar's Art Deco exterior, clean source of locomotion (electricity), smooth travel on steel rails, and bright color look and ride like nothing on the road today. By virtue of being different, they catch the eyes and the imagination. Yet PCCs are also strangely familiar to us, even for those who never witnessed them in their original context. They recall transit of a bygone era, enticing us to imagine a time when transportation was more civil both to the pedestrian and the natural environment. The longing for things and situations of the past—nostalgia—is strong with Streamliners and beckons us to board. Time, it would appear, is on their side.

San Francisco's current fleet of restored PCCs offers an interesting case study in the transformation of what was once mundane transit in this country into unique transit today. Certainly, the streamlined, Art Deco style of the PCCs is a good fit for the city, bridging Victorian and Modernist architectural styles that prevail along Market Street. But the most compelling feature of the city's Streamliners is their color—or, rather, colors. A dispute was waged during the reconditioning of these streetcars: paint them all a single scheme to reflect the city's municipal transit livery or paint them in varied schemes to represent San Francisco and other American cities that originally employed PCC cars? Thankfully, multiple liveries prevailed. Though the PCCs are virtually identical in form, their bright, wildly different paint schemes give the impression that these vehicles are very different from one another. Boston, Brooklyn, Chicago, Cincinnati, Los Angeles, and Philadelphia are just a few of the cities represented in San Francisco's Streamliner fleet. These cars, with seemingly different origins, add to the cosmopolitan flair of this already diverse city, painting the streets in a rainbow of color. Since the cabins of the Streamliners are quite utilitarian, capturing people's attention necessarily has to be done through exterior finishes. Painting the entire PCC fleet one color may have yielded a more banal fleet of transit vehicles. Multiple paint schemes add variety and interest, compelling passengers to ask themselves, "What city will I be visiting this time?"

PETER WITT TRAMS IN MILAN

Waiting for a streetcar on Market Street, a curious situation arises. It doesn't happen often—more an anomaly than an occurrence with any predictability—but on occasion a stream-lined American PCC car shores up to a densely populated transit island, with a quirky bright-orange, foreign-looking streetcar in tow. When such a rift in the transit schedule fortuitously presents itself, an interesting pattern of behavior emerges. Passengers will allow the streetcar native to Philadelphia (or Baltimore or Boston or Louisville) to pass them by and wait, instead, to board the one that hails from Milan, Italy. Why? An overcrowded Streamliner that arrives first is the answer only rarely. There is something peculiar yet compelling about these immigrant streetcars. Their form ignites a curiosity within those who are strangers to both cars, coercing them to choose European aesthetics over domestic ones. For those already familiar with the passenger cabins within both the Italian and American streetcars, the answer is obvious: what these strap-hangers already know is that, once aboard the Italian jewels, transit can be more than a planning or engineering endeavor; it can be an architectural one as well.

The design of the Milan trams is intriguing, as Peter Witt, the architect of these beguiling streetcars, hailed from America. As demand for streetcar transportation grew in this country, Witt recognized the need for a vehicle with greater passenger movement and

SPACIOUS, COMFORTABLE, AND EXQUISITELY DETAILED, THE ITALIAN-MADE "PETER WITT" TRAMS (TOP) BRIM WITH EFFERVESCENCE. THESE STREETCARS OFFER AN ENVIRONMENT AKIN TO GREAT SOCIAL HANGOUTS. MEANWHILE, THE CITY'S AMERICAN-MADE PCC STREETCARS (BOTTOM) ARE MORE ASOCIAL, WITH A SEATING ARRANGEMENT AND CABIN DECOR SIMILAR TO A TYPICAL BUS.

capacity. In 1914, Witt completed plans for a more efficient streetcar, and cities throughout the United States and Canada built cars based on his design. But it was in Milan, Italy, where Witt's design gained the most popularity. Milan built hundreds of "Peter Witts" during the late 1920s, and they still course through the streets of the city today. Peter Witt trams were never built for San Francisco, however, and all the vehicles in the city's fleet have been recently imported from Milan. Though their design may have originated in America, these immigrant streetcars exhibit subtle touches of ornament from their Italian ancestry, giving them a distinctiveness seldom seen in domestic transit.

The Peter Witt trams suggest that transit can offer more than the simple function of efficiently shuttling crowds from one place to another. The streetcar's cabin provides a welcoming environment replete with comfort, warmth, and social opportunity. The Milan streetcar exhibits the care and attention to detail usually reserved for our most beloved social hangouts, with surprising touches of home. The cabins are finished in fine, polished woods. The benches, built to the curves and proportions of the human body, are oriented not only to facilitate conversation, but to encourage it. Large, clear, single-hung windows appear as if they were designed for a house rather than a transit car. The abundant fenestration allows natural light to suffuse the cabin, while allowing passengers to gaze out dreamily to the magnificent sights along Market Street and the Embarcadero. As the sun falls toward the horizon and its rays enter the cabin without obstruction, passengers simply adjust the pull-down shades to reduce glare. Sturdy handles held by soft leather straps that dangle from brushed stainless steel rails overhead offer elegant comfort and stability to those standing. Foreign tourists conversing in their native languages as well as "exit" signs printed in Italian—*uscita*—make us all feel a bit more cosmopolitan, allowing us to forget momentarily that we are on our way to the office. We can imagine, instead, that we are on holiday en route to our next sightseeing adventure.

When the sun finally sinks into the Pacific Ocean, ornate glass refractors enshrouding individual incandescent bulbs illuminate the passenger cabin in a soft, warm glow. Especially interesting about this lighting is that something as delicate and fragile as a glass fixture can be found in a transit car; it is a touching detail, indeed, considering public space design today seems preoccupied with vandalism rather than civility. How refreshing it is to see a touch of home in the transit car. What is also noteworthy about these fixtures is that, when a decorative refractor is broken (accidents do happen), they are not necessarily replaced with the same style. Some of the refractors have a pronounced bell shape with a large diameter, while others exhibit a more constricted circumference. This is not an objectionable detail but more a curiosity that adds quirk to the overall decor.

Materials and craftsmanship, attention to detail, architecture on wheels—these and their bright orange color separate the Peter Witt trams from other forms of public transportation. They are sophisticated yet eccentric crowd-pleasers, wholly appropriate for San Francisco. Though they hearken to a time past, these wonderfully detailed street cars provide models of comfort and joy that ought to inspire transit design of the future.

BLASTING THROUGH FRANK GEHRY'S EXPERIENCE MUSIC PROJECT, THE SEATTLE MONORAIL (TOP) OFFERS A THRILLING EXPERIENCE THAT WOULD BE WELCOME IN LAS VEGAS. IRONICALLY, THE STATIONS AND MONORAIL TRAINS IN LAS VEGAS (BOTTOM) PROVIDE QUIET FUNCTION AND UTILITY WITH INCONSPICUOUS TRAVEL BEHIND THE RESORTS, WHOLLY INCONGRUENT WITH VEGAS'S "OVER-THE-TOP" AESTHETIC.

W hen monorails debuted in America, many believed they
represented the future in urban mass transit. They first
appeared at Disneyland in Anaheim, California, in 1959 (four years after
the theme park opened) and then at the 1962 World's Fair in Seattle—
venues that showcased the delight that was possible in tomorrow's
transportation design. Decades later, the elevated tracks that quietly
whisk sleek trains through the air still seem ahead of their time.

Monorails differ from other forms of transit principally in their
infrastructure. Though monorails can run at grade or even in tunnels
below ground, monorails are generally elevated forms of transit. While
other elevated rail systems require a wide platform, with a pair of
steel rails for the trains to ride upon, monorail tracks typically consist
of a single (hence, *mono*), narrow, beam-like structure made of concrete that the trains "hug" as they glide over a city's streets. The comparatively thin, single track gives the impression that its purpose is
more to guide the elevated train along its path, rather than support
the train's weight. This subtle detail, giving the perception that the
monorail floats above ground with very little support, is a principal
reason monorails seem so futuristic.

More common as amusement park transportation, monorails are
fully capable of withstanding the rigors of the daily urban commute.
Two monorail systems in America that truly provide an alternative in

urban mass transit are found in Seattle and Las Vegas. Though both systems see heavy use by visitors, these monorails prove valuable to residents and employees as well. Similar in form and function, the two systems yield very different passenger experiences, however. An examination of these two monorails helps reveal the design considerations that leave positive—and negative—impressions on riders.

SEATTLE

The monorail in Seattle, built for the 1962 World's Fair, was an experiment in modern public transit. Because the monorail was conceived largely as a showpiece for the event, the route is not extensive. There are only two stations for the monorail: one at the Seattle Center, near the iconic Space Needle, and the other at the revitalized Westlake Center, in downtown. Nevertheless, this 1.5-mile journey that takes place two-and-a-half stories above the ground is a big hit with kids and the young at heart.

Seattle's monorail was the first full-scale commercial system in the nation and, thus, an important piece of Seattle's historical development. Riding the monorail gives the passenger insight into the aspirations and technological aptitude of this innovative city during the 1960s. The innovation continues today, especially at the ever-evolving Seattle Center. The Frank Gehry-designed Experience Music Project, a titanium-skinned structure of color and organic forms that opened in 2000, offers a unique experience along the monorail's route. Gehry's design integrates the monorail by allowing the trains to pass through the building. Thus, the monorail becomes part of the architecture, giving passengers a sense of arrival and an enriched rider experience. Traveling from the Westlake station, sweeping views of downtown and the landscape beyond flood the cabins. As the monorail pierces the titanium skin of the Experience Music Project, the passengers lose all sight, as darkness enshrouds the train. Moments later, the train emerges from the titanium envelope at the Seattle Center, our vision restored with the

Space Needle in full view. Integrating architecture with transit provides an exciting climax to a short but thrilling trip, giving passengers a real sense that the monorail is more akin to an amusement park ride rather than public transportation.

The World's Fair had spawned architectural innovation within Seattle's built environment. Interestingly, the exposition coincided with the debut on September 23, 1962, of *The Jetsons*, the popular television cartoon portraying an American family living in outer space in the twenty-first century. Along with the Space Needle, the monorail helped generate a Jetson esque urban landscape, establishing an avant-garde design precedent that people were embracing at the time. Seattle has since been proud of its forward outlook and welcomes technology and design that is consistent with its innovative visions. This attitude explains why futuristic structures—such as Gehry's Experience Music Project, the Rem Koolhaas-designed downtown public library, and the new football and baseball stadiums—all feel at home in Seattle. Today, this expanded collection of engineering and architectural marvels speaks an aesthetic language that harmonizes with Seattle's visions, then and now.

The design of the monorail trains also plays an important role in enhancing the passenger experience. Consistent with the theme of the World's Fair, the monorail trains are sleek, elegant, and very modern. The numerous large, clear windows along the front, back, and sides of the train, along with the skylight windows that run the length of the train's roof, allow vast amounts of natural light into the passenger cabin, a necessity given Seattle's often dark and cloudy weather. The abundance of windows also allows for broader views, providing a better visual connection between the passenger and passing environment.

Perhaps the greatest design feature is the cabin's seating arrangement, a composition and orientation that offers choice and opportunity. The floor plan encourages casual conversation with strangers or intimate conversation with friends, as groups of seats face each other.

SEATTLE'S MONORAIL OFFERS GREAT LESSONS IN TRANSPARENCY. BOTH THE TRAIN'S CABIN (TOP) AND OPEN TRACKS (BOTTOM) ALLOW AN ABUNDANCE OF LIGHT AND SKY AND VIEWS BEYOND.

Other seats are oriented toward the side of the train, allowing passengers an unobstructed panorama without having to strain their neck. There are seats that accommodate those who prefer solitude and only wish to read or passively watch others. There are even a few seats near the ends of the train, providing grand views out the back and front and not just out the sides, as is typically the case with other public transportation. The best seats in the house, however, are the two located next to the train operator and the control panel. It is the dream of every youngster (and some adult "boys" and "girls" as well) to drive a train. The Seattle Monorail offers the closest possible experience to those with such a desire. Looking out of the front of the train through large, clear windows, seeing what the driver sees, and being able to watch as he operates the vehicle provides a truly unique experience. These seats offer the most captivating views and, hence, are a passenger's favorite.

To be able to sit at the front of the monorail train, or any vehicle, is not a trivial detail. The opportunity is commonplace in automobile design yet rare in public transit. It is the nature of passengers to want to ride shotgun—to be offered the front-seat view—regardless if the ride is in a private vehicle or a public one. People generally prefer to face forward as they move through the environment and to be given an unobstructed view of the oncoming scene. The back-seat view is seldom our first preference. Transit vehicles are often designed to provide *only* the back-seat view. It seems a shame that an opportunity for a few passengers to ride alongside the driver could not be incorporated within more public transit vehicles. The Seattle Monorail proves it is possible, and this modest design detail yields the most joyful experience to the lucky two.

The biggest challenge in elevated transit design is the overhead infrastructure and its resultant effects on the streets below. Elevated tracks can cast deep shade on the sidewalks, making it physically and psychologically uncomfortable for pedestrians. Elevated structures have severed neighborhoods, creating barriers to connectivity.

These structures are generally unsightly and are quite effective at transmitting the noise of passing trains down to the streets. Indeed, many cities that incorporate an elevated transit system realize deterioration in the quality of the street life below. As evidenced in Disneyland, it is possible to design a benign infrastructure for the elevated monorail trains, and Seattle has done so. The colonnade of relatively thin concrete columns that march down Seattle's Fifth Avenue does not create the physical barrier usually associated with elevated transit. Autos are free to maneuver about the columns—a choice that, at first, seems dangerous but actually emphasizes the inconspicuousness of the infrastructure while contributing to a unique driving experience. The structure does not separate neighborhoods, much like railroad tracks or expressways do. Visually, the openness of the elevated infrastructure doesn't impose a psychological barrier either, unlike a typical freeway overpass. Overall, the structure is surprisingly transparent, almost light and airy.

In a conversation I had with Peter Katz, author of *The New Urbanism: Toward an Architecture of Community*, he noted that Seattleites "love the damn thing. They liken it to a tree canopy."[1] The simile is apt. The overhead tracks do not block light or views but merely filter them. Their existence justifies the reward; they are a benign conduit for the delight that passes overhead every few minutes.

LAS VEGAS

In July 2004, the Robert N. Broadbent monorail opened in Las Vegas, shuttling passengers along the entire four-mile stretch of the Strip. The monorail, which consists of driverless multiple-car trains, operates on tracks thirty feet in the air, removed from the traffic congestion on the streets below. The train cars are sleek, modern, and fully air-conditioned, and they provide comfortable seating with additional room for standing. The power source is electricity, making for transit that is clean and quiet, and the cars and train stations are fully compliant with the

Americans with Disabilities Act (ADA). There are many commendable characteristics of the Las Vegas monorail, and, given the nearly thirty-five million people who visit the Strip each year, the tens of thousands of employees who work in the resorts, and the growing number of businesses and residential units that have spurted in the immediate area, mass transit is direly needed for this booming desert community.

While the intentions of the Las Vegas monorail are laudable, the system cannot be praised for the experience it offers passengers. As with any resort destination, "the experience" is the reason for the Strip's existence. The monorail in Las Vegas is a stoic effort, providing quiet function and utility—completely incongruent with the "over-the-top," "in-your-face" aesthetic of the Strip. The stations and trains lack the verve that one would expect in Las Vegas. The monorail is safe, clean, comfortable, quiet . . . but hopelessly dull. Modest changes and tweaks in individual elements of the system might enliven the journey somewhat, but the biggest obstacle is likely insurmountable: the monorail's inconspicuous location.

The development along the Strip today consists of scaled replicas of famous places throughout the world—Bellagio, Giza, Monte Carlo, New York City, Paris, and Venice—replicas that are more or less faithful in architectural detail if not in geographical context. The concept behind each resort is the re-creation of an experience—a taste of Paris, the wonders of Giza, or a romantic gondola ride for lovers through Venice. Las Vegas Boulevard, the spine of the Strip, connects these experiences, providing a direct route from New York City to Paris and on to Giza. Thus, this street is a bustling public space, providing visitors an opportunity to stroll and sightsee, to meet people and take in a free show, and to absorb wholly this spectacle in the desert.

The current monorail route, all four miles, however, runs *behind* the resort properties that define the eastern side of the Strip. Thus, the location of the monorail provides a fundamentally flawed passenger experience. Instead of being able to witness the animated street scene along

Lake Como or under the Statue of Liberty, the Eiffel Tower, or the Campanile, passengers are offered immediate views of parking lots, garages, and maintenance sheds. While it may be argued that a different view of Las Vegas is offered, one that reveals the homely and utilitarian side of the Strip necessary for the glitz along Las Vegas Boulevard, the chance to witness that side of the Strip is not the reason tourists spend their hard-earned money to vacation in Las Vegas. Successful transit is enjoyable and provides a memorable experience. The existing monorail route may provide comfortable service but little else.

The monorail's location begets other problems stemming from poor visibility. Successful transit is conspicuous to pedestrians. People need to be reminded constantly of their public transit alternatives, and a highly visible transit system makes people aware of their choices in mobility. Unfortunately, nowhere on Las Vegas Boulevard can a would-be passenger readily spot the monorail. Many have no idea the monorail exists, much less where it is or how to access it, and those who are aware of the monorail find it frustrating to get to. Since the monorail is located behind the resorts, passengers must walk *through* the casinos to access the stations. That is easier said than done. Casinos are purposely designed to make it difficult for patrons to find their way out, coercing them to put more quarters in the slot machine or to play a few more hands of blackjack in the hunt for an exit. Walking through a casino with purpose, ignoring the barrage of bells and bling-blings, is practically an exercise in futility.

Transit should provide a more efficient alternative to walking, especially if a destination exceeds a comfortable walking distance (typically about a quarter-mile). Consider the following quandary, a fairly common one on the Strip. The Statue of Liberty and the Eiffel Tower are two of the most popular and photogenic landmarks in Las Vegas. If you are outside the MGM Grand snapping pictures of the Statue of Liberty and then decide to visit the Eiffel Tower at the Paris resort up the street, you are faced with a difficult choice. One is to walk along Las Vegas

TOP: SWEEPING VIEWS AND AN OPPORTUNITY TO "CO-PILOT" THE MONORAIL THROUGH THE SKIES
OF SEATTLE YIELD AN UNFORGETTABLE EXPERIENCE. (PHOTOGRAPH FROM THE ORIGINAL 1962
WORLD'S FAIR BROCHURE, COURTESY OF KIM PEDERSEN OF THE MONORAIL SOCIETY.)
BOTTOM: MAINTENANCE SHEDS, PARKING LOTS, AND GARAGES DOMINATE THE VIEW ABOARD THE
LAS VEGAS MONORAIL.

Boulevard, but the distance between the resorts is quite far at 4,000 feet, or about three-quarters of a mile. Alternatively, you can take the monorail, since the train stops at both resorts. The distance from the street to the monorail station behind the MGM Grand, however, is 2,100 feet. After disembarking at the Bally's/Paris station, you need to walk another 1,900 feet to get back to Las Vegas Boulevard to view the Eiffel Tower. By taking transit, you still have to walk 4,000 feet! Furthermore, the fact that the monorail is behind the resort properties that border the eastern side of Las Vegas Boulevard renders the resorts along the western side without direct service. Transit should be equitable to the people and places it serves, and the Las Vegas monorail is literally one-sided.

Many of the monorail's shortcomings could be alleviated if the route were located right where all the action is, directly on Las Vegas Boulevard. Simply relocating the monorail system from its current location to the center of the Strip, however, may be a poor strategy. Any elevated transit system, monorail or otherwise, may be flawed in regards to enhancing the experience along the Strip. The elevated tracks would create an objectionable visual barrier along Las Vegas Boulevard if relocated in its present form. Unlike Seattle's Fifth Avenue, which is pleasant though not particularly noteworthy *except* for the monorail, Las Vegas Boulevard is literally the heart of the Strip, the exceptional place to see and be seen. The elevated tracks and the associated above-ground transit stations would not only ruin sight lines down the length of the street, but also diminish the all-important and unique scale of the Las Vegas Strip. The Eiffel Tower in Las Vegas is not a full-scale replica, but a half-scale version. The Strip's rendition of the Campanile, Rialto Bridge, Statue of Liberty, and Brooklyn Bridge are also reduced-scale replicas. The illusion of grandeur is predicated on the human perspective from ground level. Elevating us thirty feet in the air diminishes the impressiveness of these architectural re-creations.

An elevated transit system would also take us away from our contact with people on the Strip. Cruising is alive and well on Las Vegas Boulevard, and the catcalls are part of the experience for many. The atmosphere along the street—beautiful, scantily clad people bathed in neon, strolling amidst the hot desert air, searching for fun and frivolity—invites all to engage in a bit of hedonistic fantasy. Coaxing our otherwise timid expressions of voyeurism and exhibitionism is one of the greatest pleasures to be had along the Strip. The people on the street are every bit an attraction in Las Vegas as the resorts themselves. A transit system that disconnects passengers from pedestrians in Las Vegas is bound to have limited appeal.

There is no question that mass transit is desperately needed along the Strip, where condominium projects are booming and the majority of visitors are arriving by plane, needing a means to shuttle up and down the four-mile length of Las Vegas Boulevard. If the monorail could be extended to the airport and onto the resorts that line the western side of the Strip, it would still suffer from an ill-conceived route: thirty feet above and, on average, 2,000 feet away from the vivacity of Las Vegas Boulevard. Site-specific context is paramount to an engaging transportation experience. Regrettably, the joyful and memorable experiences that the monorails in Seattle and Disneyland bring will most certainly remain elusive in Las Vegas.

"A TALE OF TWO CITIES." THE SANTA BARBARA SHUTTLE'S OPEN, TRANSPARENT CABIN (TOP) IS INVIT-
ING AND OFFERS AN EXPERIENCE THAT ENGAGES THE SENSES. REGRETTABLY, PHOENIX'S MORE
OPAQUE SHUTTLE (BOTTOM) IS NOT SO ENTICING, ITS WINDOWS AND DESIGN BLOCKING OUT THE
SIGHTS, SOUNDS, SMELLS, AND WARM AIR OF DOWNTOWN.

CHAPTER FIVE

Shuttles in Santa Barbara, Phoenix, and Chattanooga

Shuttles are typically trackless, rubber-tired, gasoline- or electric-powered vehicles that are operated by a driver seated at the front of the vehicle. In their most basic form, they resemble small buses. When designed appropriately, shuttles not only become charming alternatives to the typical city bus, but add unique character to the animation along city streets. Many municipalities have already incorporated a shuttle system to serve a specific area within the city, such as the downtown or an historic district. Shuttles often prove more flexible and cost-effective than other types of transit, and they are well suited to the smaller scale of a single district or neighborhood.

Perhaps the most appealing characteristic of shuttles is their modest size. They are more appropriately scaled for the pedestrian, unlike the articulated buses that seem to be growing into enormous, impersonal behemoths. Shuttles provide a more intimate passenger realm, a quality that can be very compelling to the potential rider.

The shuttles used in downtown Santa Barbara, Phoenix, and Chattanooga share similar attributes. All are unique elements within the built environment and provide distinctive animation along the streets they serve. The shuttles in these three cities are more humanly scaled in overall size than a typical bus, and they all provide inexpensive, convenient methods of getting around their respective downtowns.

Santa Barbara and Phoenix are profiled because their shuttles exhibit cabin designs that are climate-responsive to their respective coastal and desert environments. This shared design response, however, delivers fundamentally different experiences for both passengers and pedestrians. Chattanooga's transit tale is bittersweet. What began with the loftiest aspirations, and the most laudable of intentions, arguably ended with a compromised passenger experience. The lessons learned from Santa Barbara, Phoenix, and Chattanooga profoundly illustrate how even the most seemingly benign transit car details can greatly affect the quality of the transit ride.

SANTA BARBARA

Santa Barbara enjoys one of the mildest climates in the nation. This central California coastal community experiences more than 300 days of sunshine a year. Average daytime temperatures range from sixty-five degrees in winter to seventy-five degrees in summer. Nighttime temperatures are also comparatively mild, with average lows of forty-five degrees in winter months and sixty degrees during summer. While rain can be heavy at times during winter months, the rest of the year is quite dry. The combined rainfall from April through October averages a scant two inches—the equivalent of Las Vegas's precipitation during the same period. The comfortable climate of Santa Barbara encourages people to "get out and about" and helps ensure vibrancy within the downtown and along the beach, regardless of season or time of day.

The shuttles that operate along Santa Barbara's Downtown— Waterfront route are a testament to the region's mild climate. The windows and doors of the passenger cabin are without glass panes, resulting in an open-air cabin design. Hence, there are no barriers between the passengers and the sights, sounds, and smells of the city. Riders are rewarded with unobstructed views of the magnificent waterfront and the bustle of downtown. A passenger can effortlessly discern the facial expressions of passing pedestrians and can even hear their conversations when the shuttle pulls over at designated stops. The fragrance of bloom-ing jasmine, the fresh Pacific Ocean air, and the aromas from the many cafés and eateries that line State Street suffuse the cabin. Though there is a roof overhead, passengers are free to stick an arm out and catch a handful of Santa Barbara's warm sunny rays. This simple design attrib-ute—what urban designers refer to as *transparency*—provides a truly sen-sual experience and proves fundamental to a passenger's enrichment.

Santa Barbara does have periods of inclement weather, and one may wonder about the viability of an open-air cabin during cold, windy, or rainy days. The solution is as simple as it is ingenious: removable window panes. Back at the transit barn, glass panes—seven for each shuttle—can be installed within the window openings in a matter of minutes, with a quick quarter-turn of a few clips. If an unseasonably warm day occurs in January, the windows are removed; if rain returns the following day, the window panes are easily re-installed. This effort-less design allows for the most finicky of weather patterns, while ensur-ing a comfortable and enjoyable ride regardless of climatic conditions. Curiously, these shuttles were never outfitted with an operable or removable door, just an opening. While some may contend that such an omission is a design flaw, the open-door cavity maintains the circulation of fresh air and city scents within the cabin. And, because even the coolest of Santa Barbara's days are hardly frigid, the conditions inside the shuttle are rarely uncomfortable.

Santa Barbara's shuttle is far from a simple shortened bus, and its design differences go beyond cabin transparency. The shuttle's exterior colors—white with simple sea-green accents—wholly harmonize with the landscape of this beach community. A modest cupola projects from the roof of the vehicle, lined with windows that gather additional light for the cabin. During holidays, the fronts of the shuttles are outfitted with festive ornaments appropriate for the occasion. Near Thanksgiving, for example, large caricatures of smiling turkeys are affixed to the roof of the shuttle, reminding pedestrians of the upcoming holiday and providing a bit of

TOP: MAGNIFICENT VIEWS OF PARADISIACAL BEACHES, FRESH OCEAN AIR, AND WARM SUNNY RAYS
ARE OFFERED LARGELY WITHOUT OBSTRUCTION ABOARD SANTA BARBARA'S SHUTTLES.
BOTTOM: CONVERSELY, THE EXPERIENCE ABOARD THE CHATTANOOGA SHUTTLE IS MORE SEDATE,
OWING TO ITS MORE "BUS-LIKE" CABIN, TINTED WINDOWS, AND LIMITED AIR CIRCULATION.

whimsy to an already cheery street scene. In many ways, the shuttle is as quirky and unique as the seaside town itself.

Santa Barbara's public transport is also among the most sociable in the nation. That is because small talk between passengers is easy, and many factors contribute to the conversation-friendly atmosphere. One is the shuttle's power source: electricity. Riders do not have to raise their voices over the rumblings of a diesel engine just to be heard. Rubber tires and the relatively silent operation of the battery-powered motor guarantee a cabin in which road noise is refreshingly absent. Leather-upholstered bench seats, arranged around the perimeter of the cabin, facilitate face-to-face interaction among the passengers. The orientation of the seating also allows passengers to survey effortlessly the passing scene.

The quietness of the shuttle, along with the seating style and orientation, together ensure comfortable conditions and social opportunity for passengers. Smiles and laughter are plentiful within this transit car, and the mirth is infectious. Spirits are high, and people seem to revel in the opportunity to share enthusiasm through verbal means. This cheerful atmosphere is refreshing and seems to bring out the best in people. During one visit, a female tourist, not possessing exact change for the fare, was not allowed to board the shuttle. "I'm sorry, but rules are rules," proclaimed the driver. The tourist's face showed obvious disappointment, but she off-boarded without objection. As the shuttle pulled away, a couple of passengers motioned for the driver to stop and asked the tourist if they could pay her fare. Because of the open-cabin design and the quiet operation of the shuttle, the passengers did not have to leave their seats for this verbal exchange nor did they have to raise their voices. The windowless cabin allowed the passengers onboard to communicate easily with the tourist on the sidewalk, and the overall design had an effect, it seems, on their mood and generosity. The tourist thanked them, boarded the vehicle, and offered the gracious passengers a dollar in exchange for coins needed for the fare box. They declined and paid her fare outright. A few seconds later, the mirth that was momentarily suspended during this friendly negotiation resurfaced, and, as the shuttle made its way down State Street, laughter could be heard.

For a city with paradisiacal beaches and downtown sidewalks lined with beautiful people, lush landscaping, and exquisite Mission Style architecture—environments that are best experienced on foot—it seems public transit would have little to offer pedestrians. Because of its extraordinary design, however, Santa Barbara's Downtown—Waterfront shuttles do not feel removed from these scintillating environments but are an extension of them. The experience is as close to Disneyland's Main Street, U.S.A. as true public transportation can get but without the entrance fees, costumes, and scripts. Make no mistake, this is a delightfully authentic experience. Indeed, even among public transportation's most discerning critics—teenagers—this seaside city's shuttle is met with approval. In cities throughout central and southern California, public transit is often scorned and considered "un-cool" by teenagers. They would rather ride skateboards, walk, or—heaven forbid—have their parents drive them around than be caught in some form of public transit. The unique exterior design of Santa Barbara's circulator, however, along with the social activity, captivating views, and perceived comfort within the shuttle, promise a rewarding and decidedly "cool" transit experience. This promise is so enticing that it succeeds in attracting people of all ages—even teenagers.

PHOENIX

Similar to Santa Barbara's Downtown—Waterfront shuttles, the design of Phoenix's Downtown Area Shuttles (DASH) is a testament to the extreme climate of its natural environment. Daytime temperatures in the Sonoran Desert can soar well above 115 degrees Fahrenheit during summer months, and, even in late spring and early fall, temperatures can reach near the century mark, making the outdoor environment uncomfortably hot much of the year. Thus, transit planners in the city desired a vehicle that could effectively shut out the region's extreme heat. Offering a respite from the sun-baked sidewalks would be necessary to attract riders, and, quite appropriately, a climate-controlled shuttle with heavily tinted and inoperable windows was chosen.

The problem with this singular approach is that the opaque and sealed environs of the cabin repel not only hot air, but the sights, sounds, and smells of the downtown as well. The heavily tinted windows of the cabin dim the otherwise vibrant colors along the downtown streets. Aromas from the many cafés and eateries are unable to enter the passenger realm. Sounds are muted by the sealed conditions within the shuttle, and there is no chance to feel the warm sun or cool desert nighttime air during the moderate months of the year. If an analogy can be drawn, the experience offered to passengers aboard the DASH is quite similar to that of an office-worker staring out from the tinted windows of his or her fluorescent-lighted, recycled air-conditioned cubicle. The experience is more sterile than stimulating.

The shuttle's opacity diminishes the experience not only for passengers, but for pedestrians (and potential passengers) as well. Unlike Santa Barbara's shuttles, which effortlessly attract people from its vibrant city streets, Phoenix's version lacks compulsion. People not only enjoy, but retrieve a good deal of information from seeing other people and their expressions. More often than not, pedestrians can witness good-humored interaction between passengers aboard Santa Barbara's shuttle, and such an atmosphere is inviting. Potential passengers in Phoenix have no idea who or how many are already on board or what social atmosphere they may be boarding onto. We tend to be more conservative emotionally when entering an unknown social situation. We are often socially defensive until we are assured the situation is agreeable. Consequently, many pedestrians may opt to pass on a shuttle ride, as the street is a relatively interesting and presumably safe environment, even if it is a bit too warm. Those who do board need time to let down their guard and feel ready to engage in small talk, should the conditions within the cabin encourage it. Since the distances people travel in the shuttle are comparatively short, the point at which we feel settled and ready to interact may never arrive.

Opacity is the most lamentable quality regarding the Phoenix DASH. Our physiological senses are shut out from the downtown experience, and there is no connection between passenger and pedestrian. Does the extreme heat of the summer months necessitate sealed and climate-controlled conditions? Or is it enough to ensure that the sun's rays are shielded from our skin but still allow outside air to flow throughout the cabin, thereby creating a cooling effect? Additionally, can't small electric fans be placed within the cabin, much like those in transit trains all over the world? It should be noted that the tops of the windows are equipped with vents—narrow panes of glass that can be opened inward for some air circulation. Their location, however, means it is difficult for passengers to open and close them and to do so only while standing. They are too high to allow passengers to feel breezes across their faces or to allow them to peer out to the passing street scene. Even if the vents were lower, transparency would not be significantly improved. The vent glass is rather small and, like the main windows, heavily tinted. And they only open a marginal amount (a crack is the most apt description). Their size, location, and limited operability do not effectively invite the sounds or smells of downtown into the cabin either. It seems there are better ways to design a modicum of permeability while keeping conditions cool inside the cabin, which could allow for a heightened user experience rather than a predominantly sealed environment that dulls our senses. Because the Phoenix shuttle responds to the desert climate in this particular manner, the experience, for both the pedestrian and the passenger, is diminished, compared to that of Santa Barbara's shuttle.

Not all is woeful about the DASH, however. Its pedestrian scale is certainly inviting, but its most captivating quality is its color. The shuttles are clad in metallic-copper paint to coordinate with the other "streetscape" elements within downtown's Copper Square. Copper Square is the city's "urban lifestyle" district: a ninety-block area with eateries, bars, markets, and cultural attractions, such as museums, theaters, and sports and music venues. As part of its downtown revitalization strategy, the city of Phoenix decided upon a theme that is tied to history and place, and it chose a color to help define and give identity to the heart of the city. The elements of the street—light standards, tree guards, banners, murals, information kiosks, and benches—are all dressed in copper and tastefully so. Though these street improvements certainly add flair to a district on the rebound, they are literally static. Of the improvements, only the shuttle is animated. The lamentable qualities aside, the modestly scaled, copper-clad DASH adds considerable and needed vitality to the streets of downtown Phoenix. With minor improvements, Copper Square's shuttle could prove that public transport in the desert can be comfortable, compelling, and memorable, regardless of the outside temperature.

CHATTANOOGA

Chattanooga is one of the great American success stories of recent time. Once labeled by the Environmental Protection Agency and Walter Cronkite on the *CBS Evening News* as the "dirtiest city in America," at a time when motorists had to turn on their headlights in the middle of the day to see through the smoke and soot, Chattanooga today is clean and green and boasts an active waterfront and a vibrant downtown that has attracted visitors and spurred economic growth throughout the city. Public transit was one of the most important elements in the success of Chattanooga's revitalization strategy, and the downtown shuttle system deserves mention for laudable intentions.

Beginning in the early 1980s, almost fifteen years after the city received its infamous moniker, Chattanooga's riverfront and downtown witnessed large-scale revitalization efforts. As part of the redevelopment process, planners began thinking about integrating public transportation into the city center, and discussions ensued as to what type of circulator would be best for Chattanooga. The city has a rich transportation history, having employed various horse-drawn vehicles, streetcars, and even a famous incline up Lookout Mountain. Of course, the most famous transport system was Chattanooga's railroad, and one might logically conclude it appropriate to pay homage to the city's brightest star, the Chattanooga Choo-Choo. Nicknamed by a newspaper columnist during its maiden voyage in 1880, the Chattanooga Choo-Choo created the first major link in public transportation between the North and the South. Sixty years later, the railroad and Track 29 were immortalized in American pop culture with Glen Miller's chart-topping song, "The Chattanooga Choo-Choo." Nevertheless, city and transportation officials desired a transit system that looked to the future and did not rekindle the past.

The decision to incorporate a transit system that does not recall Chattanooga's rich public transport history is certainly debatable, even as the city's overall transit intentions were undeniably praiseworthy. City leaders wanted a transit car that would become a fixture in the Chattanooga landscape, one in which the ride itself would be a unique experience. "The circulator," in the words of the Chattanooga Area Regional Transportation Authority (CARTA), "needed to be one of the fond memories of a visit to Chattanooga." CARTA officials agreed that the form of transit chosen "needed to be unique and innovative, visually attractive, and an attraction in and by itself."[1] These are commendable intentions, ones that succinctly illustrate the fundamental argument of this book. What Chattanooga finally settled upon, however, may have fallen short of these lofty aspirations.

CARTA officials considered many forms of transit before being ultimately intrigued by the electric shuttles that Santa Barbara employed. A trip out west confirmed for Chattanooga representatives that the experience on Santa Barbara's Downtown—Waterfront shuttle met the same objectives that were outlined by CARTA. Inspired, Chattanooga officials began working with local manufacturers to develop their own unique, innovative, and visually attractive circulator, while not straying too far from Santa Barbara's example. In the end, the vehicles created for Santa Barbara and Chattanooga have many similarities. Both Santa Barbara and Chattanooga employ downtown shuttles that rely on electricity for their sole power source; both exhibit a more pedestrian-friendly scale (indeed, Santa Barbara and Chattanooga use circulators that appear to be identical in width, length, and height); and both cities' shuttles are fitted with comfortable, upholstered bench seats arranged around the perimeter of the cabin, facilitating conversation and views through the generously sized windows. The differences between the two downtown shuttles are subtle and few, but the aggregate total of these variations equates to substantially different experiences for both the passenger and pedestrian.

One of the more obvious differences in design between the two shuttles concerns transparency. Whereas Santa Barbara's circulators roll through the downtown without the protection of window panes or a door (except during the foulest of days), Chattanooga's downtown shuttles have non-removable, dark tinted panes that seal the door and window openings. This is unfortunate, as Chattanooga possesses a comparatively mild climate, and assumedly one would enjoy access to the fresh air. It seldom snows in Chattanooga, owing to the relatively warm temperatures well into winter. Though there are periods in summer that are hot and humid, most days and evenings are quite pleasant. It seems that Chattanooga could have successfully offered an open-cabin design similar to Santa Barbara's. Though the door on the Chattanooga shuttle is operable, it is never open, except to allow passengers to board and alight. The windows are operable as well, but only half of each pane can slide open to allow for air circulation. This provides a degree of transparency if all windows are opened to their

EVEN TEENAGE PASSENGERS AGREE: SANTA BARBARA'S SHUTTLE (TOP) IS A DECIDEDLY "COOL" RIDE. CHATTANOOGA'S SHUTTLE (BOTTOM) LACKS THE WHIMSY AND COMPULSION OF ITS SIBLING IN SANTA BARBARA.

fullest extent, but such a situation is seldom seen. With regard to fenestration, Chattanooga's shuttle is more akin to the opaque Phoenix DASH rather than the permeable Santa Barbara circulator, from which it was modeled.

Perhaps the most subtle difference between the shuttles used in Santa Barbara and Chattanooga concerns the location of the vehicle's door. In Santa Barbara, passengers board through an opening located roughly in the middle of the shuttle, whereas Chattanoogans board their shuttle through a door located at the front of the vehicle. This may seem like a trivial detail, but, if an architectural comparison can be made, the experience of entering a vehicle at its center rather than at one end is akin to entering a foyer versus a hallway. In other words, it is principally a difference in the perception of spaciousness. Once aboard Chattanooga's shuttle, the only available "space" is to your left, toward the rear of the vehicle, much like a conventional bus. And like conventional buses—and hallways—this space is narrow and confined. Hop aboard the shuttle in Santa Barbara and immediately you find space all around you, with people sitting in front of you as well on both sides. Though the cabins are roughly the same size, Santa Barbara's interior feels more open spacious—whereas Chattanooga's feels constricted due to its more enclosed, linear nature. The roof of Santa Barbara's shuttle also sports a cupola ringed with windows, allowing more light into the cabin and increasing the headroom within the car. These details further contribute to the shuttles' feeling of spaciousness, even though the actual cabin space is modest at best. Contrast these details with the more opaque windows on the Chattanooga shuttle and a door that closes behind you, and it becomes clear that there can be a feeling of entrapment aboard this city's shuttle, a quality that is absent within Santa Barbara's vehicles.

Another subtle difference, and one that is most difficult to design for, concerns the scale of the vehicle as it relates to the scale of its environs. Santa Barbara's shuttle is an intimate size, and it travels through an intimate setting: they are well matched. Chattanooga's shuttle, though it, too, is intimately sized, travels along broad streets amidst tall buildings. The modest size of Chattanooga's shuttle feels a bit diminutive in its particular environment and, at times, feels lost. It is difficult to design a transit system that will be an appropriate scale throughout the varied development of an entire city. But when the service area is a smaller, more defined area, such as a downtown, it is not unreasonable to consider the scale of the surrounding built environment when choosing a circulator. The conversations and facial expressions that are effortlessly heard and recognized between passengers and pedestrians in downtown Santa Barbara owe, in large part, to the intimacy of the built environment. Such communication simply cannot be discerned in Chattanooga, owing, in large part, to the lack of intimacy with its built environment. Regrettably, verbal exchange between passenger and pedestrian may not be achievable in Chattanooga, as its downtown streets are perhaps a bit too broad, too heavily trafficked, and too noisy. But a more appropriately scaled circulator is entirely plausible, and it is worth pondering a brightly colored, double-decker shuttle, for example—perhaps with a removable or retractable roof when the weather permits—quietly rolling through the streets of downtown Chattanooga, allowing passengers and passersby to appreciate the city's numerous historic buildings and to make better eye contact with one another. That itself can be an engaging form of communication.

As noted earlier, the transit intentions of Chattanoogans were admirable and praiseworthy. Their investment in transit and their choice of electric locomotion reinforces the "green" attitude of this Southern community that is setting new standards in environmental stewardship. It is difficult to criticize such laudable efforts, especially when one sees just how far the city has come since the 1960s. Chattanooga has much to teach, but it still has a few lessons to learn in providing a wholly enriching transportation experience. The problem stems, it may seem, from CARTA officials being smitten with a circulator that works well in a particular setting and wanting to transplant, more or less, that same vehicle into a vastly different locale. In the pursuit to design a passenger carrier that is very similar to the Santa Barbara shuttle yet, at the same time, unique, the city of Chattanooga modified some small, yet key details. In the end, the city settled on a design that unfortunately looks more like a simple, shortened bus rather than the "unique and innovative" and "visually attractive" circulator CARTA officials originally set out to create.

AN AMUSED TOURIST DISCOVERED THIS TESTAMENT TO THE RESPECT AND ADMIRATION THAT NEW YORKERS HAVE FOR THEIR BELOVED YELLOW TAXICABS. IMITATION IS THE SINCEREST FORM OF FLATTERY.

CHAPTER SIX

Taxicabs in New York City

"There is a sun, a light that for want of a better word I can only call yellow, pale sulphur yellow, pale golden citron. How lovely yellow is!"

–VINCENT VAN GOGH[1]

Walk down any of Manhattan's streets, but particularly the Avenues, and one may be struck by a magnificent sight—an animated ribbon of yellow that threads its way through gray skyscrapers as far as the eye can see. Yellow, an uplifting color that evokes warmth and cheer, has been the required color for all licensed taxicabs in New York City for more than four decades. This simple mandate provides a welcome splash of color within the proverbial concrete jungle, an artificial ray of light to suffuse the sun-starved streets that lie in the skyscrapers' shadows.

Yellow has long been *the* distinguishing characteristic of New York City (NYC) taxicabs, even before the city's 1967 mandate. It seems that the origin of the ubiquitous yellow taxi stemmed largely from a marketing ploy by an astute taxicab entrepreneur. Shortly after the turn of the twentieth century, gasoline-powered automobiles were proving an effective competitor to horse-drawn public transport. Taxicab companies began to flourish, competition was fierce, and car owners were looking at ways to distinguish their vehicles from those of their rivals. John D. Hertz, an owner of a fleet of taxicabs, came across a study from the University of Chicago that identified yellow as the color most visible from long distances. Based on this evidence, Hertz painted his entire fleet of taxis yellow. The company he founded in 1915 then went on to become the most recognizable name in the taxicab industry: the Yellow Cab Company.

The success of Yellow Cab prompted other taxi companies to adopt yellow as the primary color for their cars. Perhaps the most revered taxicab in NYC throughout the twentieth century was the Checker cab. Built expressly as a vehicle for public transport, Checker taxicabs were yellow with signature black-and-white checkered trim and logos. These particular yellow cabs quickly became one of the most renowned symbols of life in the Big Apple. Then, in 1967, in an effort to help passengers distinguish between licensed taxicabs and a growing fleet of illegal "gypsy" cabs, NYC mandated that *all* medallion (licensed) taxicabs, regardless of manufacturer or company, be painted yellow. By simply regulating the color of these vehicles, it seems NYC has guaranteed that taxicabs will remain icons of public transport.

It is difficult to recall confidently the colors of Seattle's monorail trains or San Francisco's cable cars or even Disneyland's omnibuses, even though the overall form and design of these vehicles are quite memorable. These vehicles are, indeed, colored but not with hues or schemes that leave lasting impressions. It is hard to imagine that, if NYC's entire fleet of taxicabs were painted with a color more harmonious to the city streets—silver, gray, beige, or even black or white— they would possess the same iconic stature that they do today. Like London's endearing red double-decker buses or San Francisco's orange Peter Witt trams, the starkly contrasting color of NYC's yellow taxis shines bright among the myriad urban transport vehicles. As these taxis prove, such a simple design detail can give transit lasting character and vibrancy. Color is eye-catching and, in the case of NYC's taxicabs, provides a unique animated scene along the streets they travel.

If the sunshine yellow of NYC's taxicabs provides tantalizing stimulation for our eyes, it is quickly squelched by the assault on our ears. Among the physiological senses that unique transit engages, sound can be the most compelling. We often hear a transit car long before we see it. The benevolent "ding ding" of San Francisco's cable cars, the "clackety-clack" of New Orleans's streetcars, or, ironically, the refreshing absence of sound from Santa Barbara's electric shuttles are unique qualities that also lend fond memories. For NYC's taxis, their aural announcement is the crude "HONK" of the car horn, made unique by the succession of punches the cabbie thrusts at the steering wheel. While the sound of car horns is undeniably part of the sensual experience of the city, it is not an experience that elicits a sigh of endearment.

New York City officials have long sought ways to eliminate the constant barrage of taxi horns along the streets of Manhattan. Recently, signs have been erected along Manhattan's streets telling cabbies (and other motorists), "Don't Honk—$350 Penalty." The cabs are still equipped with horns and, as long as traffic is heavy in Manhattan, it seems those horns will be blared. Rather than attempt to enforce a "no-honk" ordinance, the salvo of sound emanating from taxicabs may present a unique opportunity. Like the color of the taxis, it would be an interesting gesture if the city regulated the sound of their horns as well. These sounds could further distinguish taxis from other automobile, truck, and bus traffic—grabbing one's attention but in delightful manner.

Many will argue that, while NYC's taxis attract tourists and locals alike, it is not because of the promise of a rewarding experience but rather out of sheer necessity. Indeed, many have voiced their displeasure over rude behavior and dangerous driving habits among some cabbies. The cars themselves are sometimes unkempt. Though the streets are literally flooded with the yellow two-ton machines, taxicabs are often hard to hail in Manhattan. There has also been a history of unpleasant and downright unsafe incidents that have taken place within NYC's cabs, the worst of which necessitated the installation of bulletproof partitions separating drivers from passengers. While a ride on Santa Barbara's shuttle or Seattle's monorail is almost always positive, experiences are not so consistent in the backseat of a NYC taxi. Locals seem either to love the city's taxis or hate them, and consensus regarding whether they are, in fact, wholly enjoyable may never be reached. Nevertheless, NYC's taxicabs offer unique experiences and social opportunities that cannot be found in other transit systems in the country, and these deserve mention.

Consider for a moment this account from a graduate student living in Greenwich Village. Vivi's recollection highlights some of the great qualities of NYC's taxis and some not so great:

"On Monday, I went to my new apartment building in Union Square to meet the manager to have guarantor papers signed. My guarantor is from California and happened to be in town. We waited for the M8 bus, which is usually on time, but it didn't show up. Buses never show up on important days. We walked to Seventh Avenue and hailed a cab. It was 9 a.m. so I didn't think that there would be any cabs available. This is the farce about NYC cabs. There are so many that you'd think you could flag one down in no time, but sometimes, you are waiting forever. This time, we waited literally 5 seconds before one pulled over and nearly ran over my legs. (We New Yorkers tend to stand in the street when hailing cabs . . . even when cars are rushing by.) I shouted out the corner address of our destination only to have him turn around and say that he couldn't hear me. I thought he was kidding, but he wasn't. So I shouted it again and he finally heard me.

"He made a right on 12th Street, only to be behind a garbage truck. He proceeded to honk at the truck and wave his fist at it. The poor garbage men. They have it rough here. There is a lot of honking going on in NYC, but ninety-five percent of it is from cabs.

"The cabbies always ask what route you want to take and exactly where you want to be dropped off. Most even wait until you get out and walk a bit so you are in the right area. Maybe they do this for just girls, but I appreciate it. We made it from the West Village to east of Union Square in 9 minutes. Definitely worth it. The subway is great if you need to go a long distance, but nothing beats the rush of flying down NYC streets and checking out the view from above ground."[2]

Vivi's experience is one that we often see re-enacted in movies and television; entertainment that gives us insight into the unique encounters that take place in the backseats of NYC's taxis. Interestingly, these media accounts usually do not have to be exaggerated for dramatic or comedic purposes, as these scenes are really not that different from the daily occurrences one might expect to find. Taxis whooshing through the streets of Manhattan, or a cabby violently shaking his fist in the air while blaring the car's horn when traffic impedes his forward movement, are experiences we've all seen in New York—even for those who have never set foot in the city.

While many Americans have vicariously experienced a few of these incidents through media entertainment, television, or cinema, they simply cannot portray accurately the visceral experience of the taxicab passenger. Cruising the streets of a magnificent city within the intimate and relatively comfortable confines of a car provides a thrill most Americans take for granted. For the many Manhattan residents who do not own cars, only the city's taxis can offer this experience. Using taxis for public transport also has the environmental benefit of not requiring vast amounts of ancillary real estate that private automobiles do. In her seminal account of the destruction of American cities wrought by the automobile, Jane Holtz Kay notes:

"Time after time, I have witnessed environments become asphalt encrusted as the urge to hold the cars of shoppers or homeowners has taken primacy. Despite better intentions, it has become apparent that an almost mathematical inevitability lies behind such design . . . . At rest, the automobile needs three parking spaces in its daily rounds—one at home, one at work, and one in the shopping center."[3]

Taxicabs, on the other hand, are great for cities that do not want or are incapable of providing the parking spaces Kay contends are necessary for the private auto. Taxis help discourage the building of parking lots, garages, strip malls, and drive-thrus, since these cars remain on the street, with little need to travel off the public realm and onto private property. Though taxis are generally confined to city streets like buses and streetcars, they can travel down alleys, highways, or even onto the occasional driveway and, thus, offer a freedom to riders that other forms of transit do not. Taxi routes are not predetermined, and this flexibility in mobility is an appealing alternative to passengers.

Taxicabs can also be sociable environments, because the operation of this form of transport is initiated through verbal exchange. Unlike most mass transit systems, where passengers can be transported to their destinations without ever having to utter a single word to the driver, the taxicab requires verbal communication. Upon entering, the cab driver asks the passenger for his or her destination, and the passenger responds. This interlude, albeit brief, can set the tone for casual conversation. Indeed, it often feels more awkward *not* to speak in the cab than to engage in small talk. And, for whatever reason, New Yorkers are at ease talking to cab drivers about the most personal matters of their lives. Much like bartenders, New York cabbies often take on the role of armchair therapists. This has inspired a few colorful personalities to extend their informal cab advice outside the realm of the taxi. One cab driver, in a spoof of the popular advice column "Dear Abbey,"

"AN ARMY OF YELLOW." IN APPARENT MILITARISTIC FORMATION, A SQUADRON OF CROWN VICTORIA CABS (TOP) MARCH DOWN FIFTH AVENUE IN MANHATTAN WHILE PEDESTRIANS NAVIGATE THROUGH EDDIES OF YELLOW AT A PARK AVENUE INTERSECTION (BOTTOM).

has an online version titled "Dear Cabby." In addition to fielding questions regarding NYC's taxi service, architecture, and history, "Dear Cabby" offers advice on relationships as well. It is obvious from the questions and comments posted on the Website that many of his inquirers were once passengers in his cab. Another taxi driver, Ahmed Ibrahim, offers pro bono matchmaking services for his passengers. Ibrahim began offering this unusual extracurricular service in response to the many complaints his fares had voiced over the difficulty of meeting people in the city. Crying, fighting, and broken hearts were commonplace in his cab, according to Ibrahim, and he felt he could offer assistance for those seeking a soul mate. After all, he meets dozens of new people every day, and, given the social nature of taxicabs, he gets to know some of his fares quite well.

Ahmed Ibrahim is certainly one of the more colorful cab drivers. In addition to his matchmaking services, he sends birthday cards to passengers, hands out roses on Valentine's Day, and decorates his cab with lights and ornaments during Christmas. What is perhaps most interesting is that Ibrahim, an immigrant from the Middle East, actively indulges in these decidedly Western traditions. In many ways, Ibrahim's embracement of American culture exemplifies the profound melting pot that is New York City. Ethnically, New York is a magnificently diverse city, and this ethnic mix is, perhaps, best reflected in the cab drivers. Besides the yellow color of the taxis, the virtual United Nations of countries and languages that are represented by NYC cabbies is the most publicized—and celebrated—characteristic of this form of public transport. From the Middle East to the Far East, the West Indies to the Indian subcontinent, Africa to Russia, NYC's cab drivers come from a plethora of exotic places. Many passengers may never have an opportunity to visit these places, but they can learn about them firsthand from former residents. There is little wonder why New Yorkers are often regarded as being among the most cosmopolitan and socially tolerant citizens in the nation.

While a cab ride through other American cities may provide a rather banal experience, in New York City, immersed in the shadows of skyscrapers and the bustle along Manhattan's streets, an opportunity to learn more about a culture and a country different from one's own is an engaging offer. And, unlike other American cities, in New York the difficulty of hailing a cab begets yet another unique social opportunity. Sharing a taxi with a stranger is commonplace in Manhattan simply because, as Vivi noted, there never seem to be enough cabs for those in need. New Yorkers feel much more at ease sharing a cab with strangers, perhaps because each is sympathetic to the plight of the other. Nobody likes being passed up by public transportation, and sacrificing what was fleetingly to be a more self-indulgent and private transport experience certainly fulfills one's good deed for the day. This benevolent gesture allows unfamiliar transit passengers an opportunity to get to know one another, and such an introduction can help build a sense of community. In the big city, where it is easy to be anonymous (even if one does not desire anonymity), it can be very difficult to meet new people. This social frustration is, perhaps, why Ibrahim's matchmaking services work so well in the taxicab. Sharing an intimate, enclosed space with a stranger, someone with whom you might literally rub shoulders, provides a prime opportunity for small talk. The absence of speech in such a situation yields an extremely awkward, uncomfortable silence, an experience we have all felt at one time or another in an elevator, for example. Light conversation helps ease this tension, and New Yorkers, perhaps because of the difficulty of making new acquaintances in the city, seem more eager to socialize. It does not happen as much on the subway, where it is easy to mind one's business, even if it is crowded. In the back of a NYC taxicab, however, two people, sharing the same space and, perhaps, even going to the same place, may have something in common, and that commonality could be worth exploring after the ride is over.

With the recognition of the social opportunities and visceral thrills that are possible inside a NYC taxicab, it is time to consider a vehicle design that best exploits these experiences. As of this writing, New York City has more than 12,000 yellow medallion (licensed) taxicabs, and ninety percent of the fleet is comprised of that omnipresent municipal vehicle, the Ford Crown Victoria. While the Crown "Vic" is functional, the vehicle design is neither exciting nor is it unique to New York. Many agree that the experience of traveling *on* NYC's streets is better than *under* them, but the Crown Vic's windows are diminutive compared to other transit vehicles. As such, the vehicle does not offer passengers particularly grand views of the city, and the exhilarating experience of being able to witness the full height of Manhattan's skyscrapers is simply impossible in the backseat of a taxi. Group socialization is also constrained with the cabin design of the Crown Victoria. While the cabin may be fine for a single passenger or a couple, a three- or four-person group cannot comfortably communicate with each other. Unlike London's black and maroon taxicabs or even New York's once-ubiquitous Checker cabs, the Crown Victoria is not designed to be a public transport vehicle. This realization is eloquently summed up by landscape architect Deborah Marton, the executive director of the not-for-profit group Design Trust for Public Space. In an interview with *The New York Times*, Marton noted:

> "In a perfect world, the taxi would be a purpose-built vehicle, designed to be a taxi, just as a post office vehicle is designed to deliver mail. If you were to design a taxi to its Platonic essence, it would not be the Crown Victoria. It serves its purpose, but it's been pushed to the limit of its efficacy as a taxi vehicle."[4]

Paul Goldberger, the esteemed architecture critic for *The New Yorker* and a former Dean of the Parsons School of Design, also recognized the Crown Victoria as being woefully miscast in the taxicab role.

He adds, "What we do is take cars, and not even particularly good cars at that, paint them yellow and put a meter in them."[5]

Design Trust for Public Space, along with the organizing efforts of Goldberger, brought together architects, designers, city officials, and even cab owners and drivers to brainstorm about what the future of taxi transport may be. Ideas offered were child car seats and wider doors for wheelchair users, thereby making the taxicab a safer and more accommodating mode of transport for a wider population. Sun roofs and front passenger seats that face the rear of the car could help improve the experience of the ride, allowing better views and a more socially engaging environment. The ideas were vast and varied, and most represented sound strategies for creating a more positive transportation experience in New York City. Mayor Michael R. Bloomberg publicly admitted that his taxi fleet is in dire need of an update. Bloomberg was not questioning the Crown Victoria's efficacy as a taxi vehicle, as Marton suggested; rather, it is the Crown Vic's poor fuel efficiency that prompted the mayor's admission. Addressing the ill economic and environmental effects caused by the gas-guzzling Crown Vics, which get a paltry fourteen miles to the gallon, Bloomberg vowed to have "the largest, cleanest fleet of taxis anywhere on the planet."[6] On May 22, 2007, Mayor Bloomberg ordered the entire fleet of taxicabs to operate on fuel-efficient hybrid engines by 2012. The list of approved vehicles for NYC's new hybrid fleet—a range of models from Toyota, Saturn, Lexus, Honda, and others—only included one Ford, and it wasn't the Crown Vic. It seems the Crown Victoria's reign has come to an end.

While there will be a greater diversity of hybrid taxicabs on the streets of Manhattan—compacts, minivans, SUVs, and sedans—they are still standard automotive models, designed for private passenger travel and not for public transport. A paradigmatic shift in taxi design, of course, will take time, and many design battles will be waged. Economics will play a major role, as will the personal wishes of the vastly influential cab owners and drivers themselves. What is most important is that a few influential designers and transportation decision-makers in New York City have recognized the transit vehicle as public space and understand that the design of the transit system is paramount to the experience afforded the passenger. While it isn't clear what the future holds for the design of NYC's iconic taxicabs, one thing seems certain: they will be yellow.

CHAPTER SEVEN

Funiculars in Pittsburgh

"Standing atop Mount Washington, the steep hill that rises giddily on the city's south side, sightseers enjoy the unforgettable panorama of the Allegheny and Monongahela rivers flowing together to create the mighty Ohio, that waterway so essential in the nation's settlement."

—*USA WEEKEND MAGAZINE*[1]

There is no disputing that the view from the bluffs of Mount Washington toward Pittsburgh's river-cradled downtown is nothing short of spectacular. It is a miraculous blend of human achievement set in a stunning geography. Soaring skyscrapers built within a bow-shaped park seem to float atop a valley of water, moored to the forested river bluffs with playful suspension bridges. What is most surprising is that there are few places on Mount Washington where one can witness this unforgettable panorama, except from public transit. Grandview Avenue, the once aptly named street that runs atop the bluffs of Mount Washington, is today lined with private residences, businesses, and restaurants—buildings that, along with the overgrown brush, obstruct the stunning view from the sidewalk. Overlooks have been constructed to remedy the diminishing views, but these do not offer a vantage point that puts the confluence of the Allegheny, Monongahela, and Ohio rivers and the "Golden Triangle" in full view. That postcard panorama is best seen from the transit plaza of the

TOP: A POSTCARD PANORAMA OF DOWNTOWN PITTSBURGH, AS VIEWED FROM THE TRANSIT PLAZA
OF THE DUQUESNE INCLINE.
BOTTOM: THE SPACIOUS AND HANDSOMELY DETAILED WOODEN CARS FRAME BREATHTAKING
VIEWS OF THE "GOLDEN TRIANGLE" AT THE CONFLUENCE OF THE ALLEGHENY, MONONGAHELA,
AND OHIO RIVERS.

Duquesne Incline and from within the funicular cars themselves. The historic charm and picture-perfect views afforded from the funicular make this unique public transportation system a popular attraction in the Steel City.

Funiculars are inclined cable railways comprised of just two passenger cars. Like the cable cars of San Francisco, funiculars are an invention borne from topographical constraint. Their purpose is to transport people up and down the sheer faces of hills, mountains, and river bluffs—insurmountable obstacles for most transit systems. Unlike cable cars, which grip and release a constantly moving cable, funiculars are permanently attached to their line. Thus, the passenger cars cannot move independently of each other, as they do in San Francisco. The cable that attaches the two passenger cars runs through a pulley at the top of the incline. As one car glides down the hill, its weight helps pull the other one up, and the two cars pass each other mid-route. This counterbalance is what distinguishes funiculars from other forms of cable transit.

Funiculars were found in many American cities a century ago. These inclined cable railways transported people from their homes on top of a hill or bluff to the shopping or business district below. Those funiculars that remain in operation today, such as the Angel's Flight Railway on Bunker Hill in Los Angeles, the Lookout Mountain Incline in Chattanooga, and the Fenelon Place Elevator in Dubuque, Iowa, still provide unique and delightful rides, but they are almost exclusively used by tourists. Only in Pittsburgh, where funiculars gained the largest acceptance, do commuters still rely on this hillside transit.

Pittsburgh has operated seventeen passenger funiculars (or "inclines," as they are referred to in the city) throughout its history. The desire for residential development beyond the river flats to the surrounding bluffs demanded a transit system that could efficiently connect hilltop residents to business and industry 400 feet below. On May 28, 1870, the Monongahela Incline opened, encouraging vigorous development on Mount Washington. The incline proved so popular that a dozen more were built before the end of the nineteenth century. While funiculars enjoyed an incomparable popularity in Pittsburgh and proved a logical means to traverse the steep river bluffs, they could not compete with the technological innovation that was revolutionizing transit at the time. One by one, Pittsburgh's funiculars succumbed to the electric streetcar. Even though funiculars still provided the most direct route from the bluffs to the river's edge, the technology was considered obsolete and ridership plummeted. Only two funiculars survived the advance of the streetcar and, later, the automobile: the Monongahela and the Duquesne inclines, historic icons of travel in Pittsburgh today.[2]

The city's two funiculars are almost identical in form and function, and both deliver memorable experiences but in dissimilar ways. The Duquesne Incline is a labor of love, rescued from near abandonment in 1963. The Society for the Preservation of the Duquesne Heights Incline, a not-for-profit enterprise "dedicated to the preservation of that which cannot be replaced," operates and maintains the transit system without any government subsidies, relying heavily on passenger fares, memberships, and donations.[3] This is a tall order, considering the funicular maintains a commuter schedule despite the few commuters who actually use the system today. Unlike many visitor attractions, which often operate seasonally and even then with limited hours, the Duquesne Incline is open every day, including holidays, from early morning until well after midnight. The reclamation effort in 1963 was spearheaded by commuters for commuters, although those numbers dwindled during the ensuing decades. In the face of declining ridership and tight funds, Jim Presken, the society's vice president, is adamant about keeping the hours of operation open to serve commuters, regardless of how few there are. "We only get one or two commuters at 5:30 in the morning," he explains, "but to shorten the hours goes against our mission."[4] That mission is to give residents on Mount

Washington a choice in mobility, a mission that the impassioned staff tirelessly upholds with little monetary reward.

Once onboard the Duquesne Incline, the reason for such impassioned preservation is evident. The funicular's cars are like nothing in transportation today. Hand-carved cherry panels with bird's-eye maple trim and amber glass transoms that ring a cupola atop a barrel-vaulted roof together create a spacious compartment of exquisite detail. Comfortable wooden benches and large clear windows line the perimeter of the cabin, providing a sociable environment that frames unforgettable panoramas. The car feels less like a transit vehicle and more like a room in a Victorian-era home. It is a very sociable space, and the unique form of the cars and compelling views from within easily spark conversation between strangers. The ride is casual, an easy journey up and down a treacherously steep bluff. Children find the steep drop in elevation exhilarating, though some adults get a bit uneasy. Any discomfort fades quickly once the city's skyline enters the cabin, commanding attention and mesmerizing all.

The view from across the river is equally entrancing. Sitting along the grand fountain that punctuates the apex of the Golden Triangle, it is easy to while away the better part of a Sunday afternoon. Children play about the fountain, joggers surpass dog walkers, and sculls and barges float by amidst shrieks of joy when the Steelers or Pirates score. And, in the distance, two bright red boxes quietly slip up and down a forested bluff. Of all the animation that takes place around the Golden Triangle, the funiculars of the Duquesne Incline seem the most amazing. Yet, just when you think you have never seen a transit system with so much quirk and charm, somebody points to another less than a mile away along the same river bluff.

The Monongahela Inclined Plane (or "The Mon," as locals efficiently refer to it) offers a distinct experience from the Duquesne Incline. The Mon is under the operation of the Port Authority of Allegheny County, a large public transit organization that provides transportation services throughout the region. The stations and cars of The Mon have been upgraded and renovated more frequently than the Duquesne, the benefit of having county, state, and federal funds to supplement passenger fares. Though The Mon seems to be in a better state of repair, in some ways it lacks the charm of the Duquesne Incline. This is most noticeable in terms of the two systems' passenger cars. The Duquesne cars are more intricately detailed, with the preserved woodwork offering distinction and architectural appeal. The Mon has a noticeable "public works" feel, lacking the original ornament and materials that are so compelling in the Duquesne.

The configuration of the passenger cars is also strikingly different. The Duquesne Incline feels communal, with people sitting casually around one large passenger compartment—similar to people seated in a living room around a coffee table. The Mon's cars, on the other hand, are divided into three separate "stair-stepped" compartments that match the slope of the incline's tracks. Sub-dividing the passenger car in this way not only diminishes the overall feeling of spaciousness, but limits outward views as well. Seating within each compartment is comprised of two opposing benches, placed barely thirty inches apart. This orientation and proximity of seating can be uncomfortable if the compartment is full, as people cannot sit across from one another without knees or feet touching. There is a fine line between a space that is intimate, promoting eye contact and casual conversation with strangers, versus one in which our personal space is violated. A minor intrusion into one's personal space is generally tolerable and, in many cases, even sparks small talk to defuse the slight awkwardness. If the intrusion is too great, we tend to shut down, internalize, avert our gaze, or fiddle with our clothing or cell phone. The Duquesne's cars feel "right" in terms of passenger orientation and proximity to one another. Rubbing shoulders with one stranger while looking at another is somehow more comfortable than if our legs are entwined with someone's whose face

TOP: THE MONONGAHELA INCLINE ("THE MON") CONNECTS RESIDENTS IN THE APARTMENTS ABOVE TO RESTAURANTS AND RETAIL ESTABISHMENTS BELOW.

BOTTOM: THE MULTI-LEVEL MONONGAHELA CARS DO NOT OFFER THE VIEWS, RICH DETAIL, OR PERCEPTION OF "SPACIOUSNESS" OF THE DUQUESNE FUNICULAR. STILL, THE RIDE IS UNIQUE.

is squarely in front of ours. The individual, smaller compartments within The Mon are just a bit too tight. In other forms of transit, this would lead to an unbearable awkwardness among passengers. Such uneasiness is averted in The Mon, thankfully. The joy of the ride and the magnificent views seem to lighten everyone's mood aboard this funicular. Though silence is prevalent within a compartment of strangers, there is still something subliminally communicative about sharing a great experience with others who undoubtedly find it as pleasurable as you.

Emerging from quaint bungalows, the quirky, brightly colored cars slowly sliding up and down green bluffs on old rail trellises give both the Duquesne and Monongahela inclines a bucolic, almost rural character. But Pittsburgh is a big city, and the dichotomy of rural and urban is most noticeable aboard The Mon, giving this funicular positive distinction over the Duquesne Incline. Unlike the Duquesne, which sees only moderate use by residents, The Mon is heavily patronized by commuters. The area atop Mount Washington surrounding The Mon is a more economically diverse neighborhood with higher density than the one surrounding the Duquesne. College students, grade school children, and the elderly overwhelm tourists at times aboard The Mon. These residents rely on the funicular to take them from their hilltop homes to destinations along the river flats. The Mon has also proven adaptable to changing times, as one car has been reconfigured to accommodate wheelchairs, bicycles, and baby strollers. The heavy use by such a diverse resident populace gives The Mon a decidedly urban feel and a publicness that is indicative of great social spaces.

Though the route is limited, The Mon is an effective mode of transportation principally because it connects residents to entertainment venues and to other transit options. It seems that the primary reason residents do not utilize the Duquesne Incline for commuting is simply because there is little to connect them to. While restaurants and residents abound near the Duquesne Incline's Mount Washington station, the lower station deposits passengers in a vacant lot within a forgotten industrial area along the river. There is a bus line that one can transfer to, but the stop is located along a high-speed, noisy arterial—an entirely unfriendly environment. The Mon connects Mount Washington residents to Station Square, a once industrial area along the river flats that is now a bustling complex filled with restaurants, shops, nightclubs, plazas, and historic charm. It is a great place to people-watch and sightsee. For those looking for an afternoon or night out, this limited route is long enough. If downtown is the destination, The Mon provides connections to the greater transit network. From the bottom station, passengers can get to downtown by catching a bus, hopping on the "T" light rail, biking, or simply walking across the Monongahela River over the historic Smithfield Street Bridge, a pleasant, scenic stroll that many people enjoy. While the Duquesne Incline arguably provides a more pleasurable ride with finer views, a relaxed space, and richer detail, The Mon remains a more practical conveyance for residents who rely on public transit to get them to their places of work, study, and entertainment.

The longevity of Pittsburgh's inclines yields a cogent point in transportation design: people crave unique experiences regardless of their purpose or destination. Commuters need transit, but visitors choose it. Though the Monongahela and Duquesne inclines exist to serve commuters, their appeal to visitors give these systems economic stability. This is an important lesson regardless of the transit system. Transit should be designed to appeal to a diverse populace and to provide a "fun-for-the-entire-family" experience. This may mean a route that is seemingly not the most logical, a form that is more playful rather than pragmatic, or a system that may cost substantially more upfront but will ultimately pay for itself because of high visitor demand or will contribute to the economic vitality of the neighborhoods it serves. Both the Mon and Duquesne inclines will remain successful, because they deliver delightfully unique experiences. It is rare when public transit offers its passengers a perspective that neither motorists nor pedestrians can share, and that is what makes Pittsburgh's inclines special.

Transit that travels on streets affords passengers the same view as pedestrians, bicyclists, and motorists. The bluffs along the Monongahela River are so sheer that it is impossible to pave a roadway down their faces. Even a staircase would prove difficult for pedestrians to negotiate easily. The funiculars navigate the grade with grace and charm, and they reward the passenger with an infinite array of subtly changing panoramas, as the cars slowly ascend hundreds of feet above the river's edge. Such views would certainly be the highlight of any commute.

CHAPTER EIGHT

Aerials and Elevateds in New York City and Chicago

T he future of public transportation, many believe, lies in the ability to whisk passengers to their destinations far above traffic-choked streets. Proponents of elevated transit also argue that routes do not have to conform to a rigid street pattern below. Where allowable, the tracks can take diagonal shortcuts through blocks—even through build-ings—in an effort to boost efficiency and reduce travel time.

Though many still envision cars and trains traveling high above city streets as a Space Age form of public transport, the idea of divorcing mass transit from the often crowded surface streets is not new to the twenty-first century. Proposals to run transit above city streets were prominent in America as far back as the mid-nineteenth century. New York City (NYC) began operating an elevated rail in 1870, serving Greenwich Street and Ninth Avenue in Manhattan.[1] Chicago began its "El" (elevated railroad) service shortly after in 1892. The monorail appeared first in Disneyland in 1959 and then debuted as true public transportation during the World's Fair in Seattle in 1962. Taking the familiar ski gondola and retrofitting it within an urban context, NYC took elevated transit to new heights with a new twist in 1976. The computer-controlled "people-movers" are the latest chapter in elevated transit in America. Common in airports throughout the world, people-movers as a mode of mass transit debuted in Miami and Detroit during the mid-1980s. These driverless, fully automated cars zip along concrete tracks

TOP: ROOSEVELT ISLAND'S CHERRY-RED GONDOLAS DANGLE PASSENGERS HIGH ABOVE THE STREETS OF MIDTOWN MANHATTAN.

BOTTOM: THE QUEENSBORO BRIDGE BLOCKS WHAT COULD HAVE BEEN A SPECTACULAR VIEW OF THE EAST RIVER AND LOWER MANHATTAN.

high above city streets, ominously suggesting that the human conductor may be an endangered species.

Two elevated systems are profiled in this chapter. Chicago's El (now sometimes referred to as the "L"), the oldest continually operated elevated transit system in the nation, illustrates a serendipitously rich social experience atop a historically significant though, arguably, woeful transportation infrastructure. The Roosevelt Island Tramway in NYC offers a new idea on elevated public transportation. Conceived merely as transitional transportation—a temporary means to cross the East River until subway service to Manhattan was to be established a few years later—the aerial tram has proven staying power. Aerial trams provide an ideal solution in public transportation when faced with challenging geographical constraints. The most "elevated" of the elevated transit systems, aerial trams can reward passengers with breathtaking views and a unique perspective on the landscape, giving them appeal to visitors and residents alike.[2]

NEW YORK CITY

Few familiar with New York City are aware of another "long island" that splits the East River into two channels. Roosevelt Island—a narrow, two-mile-long island between Manhattan and the borough of Queens—is home to some of the most underappreciated and affordable real estate in Manhattan. With a history as old as the city itself, it is interesting that Roosevelt Island has remained largely underdeveloped. But, as demand for growth is exceeding available real estate in the borough, Roosevelt Island is finally catching the eyes of developers. It is attractive because of its historic landmarks, close proximity to Midtown, and spectacular views of the Manhattan skyline. And, while residential development on the island benefits from subway and bus connections direct to Midtown, it is really Roosevelt Island's unique form of public transit that is vying for the attention of tourists and speculators alike.

It was in 1976 that another splash of color was added to NYC's public transit palette: not the sunshine yellow that is reserved for the city's taxicabs but the Roosevelt Island Tramway, a cherry-red gondola that glides on cables, suspended high over the East River. The system was designed to overcome the constraints of geography, much like the funiculars of Pittsburgh and the cable cars of San Francisco. Unlike those public transit systems, the tram was never intended to become a permanent fixture in its landscape. Borne of frustration over the New York City Transit Authority's unsuccessful attempts to provide subway service to the island, the tramway was conceived largely as an interim transit solution. Once subway service was finally established to the island in 1989, thirteen years after the tramway was constructed, the aerial tram had proven too popular with commuters to warrant its departure.[3]

The tram—really a ski gondola taken out of its alpine context and placed amid the concrete and steel peaks of Manhattan—is quite unique as a public transit vehicle. The flat-bottomed, cherry-colored box holds about 125 passengers, all but a half-dozen or so required to stand. Its large, open cabin design allows people to board easily even with bikes, wheelchairs, baby strollers, or grocery carts. In many ways, the Spartan interior provides the convenience that is so necessary to the daily needs of commuters. Its speed is modest, sixteen miles-per-hour, and the ride short, as the tram only has to traverse 3,100 feet. But it is not the horizontal path of travel that captivates riders but rather its vertical ascent. The tram summits 250 feet above the East River, promising a magnificent view of the Manhattan skyline, a promise that is largely unmet.

It is September 1, 2006, the day the Roosevelt Island tram resumes service after a five-month hiatus, and people are eager to ride again. There had been much anger and concern over the length of inoperability, most notably because the alternative transit choices between Midtown Manhattan and Roosevelt Island left little to be desired. As one passenger complained, "We are all very weary of the daily struggles and lack of options since the spring and [are] looking forward to the pleasant 3 minute crossings once again."[4] Anticipation is high today, and passengers clamor aboard. The operator follows, stepping up onto a little stand to operate the tram. He has a microphone to communicate to passengers, though one wonders if this is really necessary. The gondolas are generous in size but still smaller than even the most diminutive NYC studio apartment. The operator closes the door, leans into the microphone, and, with a linguistic efficiency that befits true New Yorkers, issues the following greeting: "Hold on." Though many may have expected a more ceremonious announcement after such a lengthy delay in service, those two words, delivered with the slightest trace of sarcasm, were entirely appropriate.

After the morning rush hour, when things return more or less to normal, parents with children begin boarding. Children are interesting to watch, because they provide unmistakable clues to the joys of life's experiences. They take these experiences at face value and wear their emotions on their sleeves. Children do not rationalize an experience the way adults do, and, if an experience is particularly fun (or boring), children let you know—if not verbally, then through their facial expressions and actions. The ride is pleasant, though nothing special. Suspended twenty-plus stories over the East River one would think "the willies" would abound. Not so. In fact, a quick glance at the expressions on the children's faces shows neither incredulity nor anxiety. Something is missing, and a legitimate guess would be a more revealing view.

Gondolas typically, by their nature, deliver breathtaking views, and one would think that a gondola ride over the East River toward Manhattan would yield fantastic panoramas of Midtown south to the skyscrapers of the financial district. Indeed, the Chrysler Building can be seen along with the Empire State Building and other Midtown icons, but the views are generally obscured. The aerial tram possesses many of the great qualities necessary for a compelling and memorable transit experience but suffers from a location too near a looming behemoth of metal that partly spoils the view. The tram runs in the shadow of the

Queensboro Bridge, barely thirty yards from this steel-trussed relic of the early 1900s. It is not a bridge of architectural beauty or grace, and its ability to snatch light and obstruct sightlines renders the view from the aerial tram to be disappointing. As one passenger succinctly noted, "You can't really see anything, other than that rusty old bridge."[5] Though one is given a completely unobstructed view north to the Upper East Side and the northern half of Roosevelt Island, the soaring human achievement of lower Manhattan and Midtown is what people want, and would pay good money, to see.

The people of Roosevelt Island are striving to boost amenities for its residents and visitors alike. Given the geographic constraints of the island, connectivity to the greater city is obviously essential to garner the interest of visitors and developers. The Roosevelt Island Operating Corporation (RIOC), an organization formed to manage, maintain, and develop the area, understands that, of the various transportation systems serving the island, the aerial tramway is the most popular. RIOC promotes the tram as a unique experience and a "must-see" for visitors in an effort to attract more people to Roosevelt Island. Through these promotional efforts, the tram has become the icon of the island. The aerial tramway is incorporated in RIOC's logo, it figures prominently on the organization's Website, and it is heavily touted as a great location for cinematography. Indeed, the aerial tram has played host to scenes in a few feature films, perhaps the most notable being the climactic battle in the 2002 movie *Spider-Man*. Of all the locations on Roosevelt Island that have appeared in film and television, RIOC boasts that "by far the single most sought-after location on Roosevelt Island is also its most unique form of transportation: The Aerial Tramway."[6] Regardless of RIOC's promotional efforts, the passenger counts throughout the day reveal that, after twenty years in service and numerous appearances in both film and photography, the tram is not the visitor must-see that one might assume. Usage is heavy during the morning and evening commute but quite sparse during the night and other periods. Other than the evening commute, it seems more people are always going to Manhattan than coming back, a sign that what draws in tourists are the things to see and do in Manhattan, rather than the tram.

Creating a transit system that is an attraction in itself, regardless of its point of origin or destination, could provide that boost in visitor and developer interest that RIOC desires. It is what transportation planners set out to do in Chattanooga, and it works in Santa Barbara as well as in New Orleans, San Francisco, and Seattle. Simply put, people are often drawn to the experience of a good ride, and neighborhoods that are served by a noteworthy transit journey often flourish. When visitors on these memorable forms of transit arrive at the terminus, most do not simply turn around and go back. Instead, they feel compelled to explore the area around the transit stop, hopefully parting with a bit of their disposable income. In these cases, transit can act as the hook by generating excitement over the ride itself.

For Roosevelt Island, the aerial tram could have provided that hook—the draw being a million-dollar view. An expansive view is a rare treasure in Manhattan, as the throngs who can wait in line for hours each day for a trip to the top of the Empire State Building can attest. Sure, some want the experience of being on top of what once was the tallest building in the world, but primarily people are eager to witness the sweeping view of countless concrete mesas and the landscape beyond, a view that pedestrians in the urban canyons below simply do not have. Obviously, the tram doesn't come close to the dizzying heights of the Empire State Building, but couldn't the journey nonetheless provide scenery worthy of a half-dozen camera clicks during that three-minute ride? With the Queensboro Bridge in the immediate foreground blocking the best sightlines, the transit journey is far from photogenic.

The aerial tramway serves a viable and much needed function, principally to get the residents of Roosevelt Island to and from Manhattan, where they work and play. And many will contend that, compared to the bus and subway, the aerial tram is the most pleasant. But the ride could be better. There are numerous factors to consider when designing and implementing any transit system. Many factors share priority and importance, and, thus, it can be difficult to find a point of beginning. Passenger enrichment, regardless of the transit system being proposed, should always be a priority and makes for an excellent beginning point. The breathtaking views of the Manhattan skyline could have been the impetus for the tram's exact location and ultimate ascent. Such a sweeping panorama is an opportunity seldom found in New York City, and the aerial tram had great potential to seize the occasion. Because the aerial tram is but a stone's throw of that "rusty old bridge," which dominates the southerly view for most of the journey, that occasion is never presented.

Nevertheless, the tram is the signature feature of Roosevelt Island and the preferred choice for transport by visitors and commuters alike. It offers valuable lessons in potentially memorable and joyful transit opportunities. The greatest thrill that aerial trams offer the passenger is a bird's-eye perspective of the landscape. Such an expansive view allows us to discern better the unique geography of a particular city, its settlement patterns, and individual architectural achievement. Ironically, a transit system that removes us physically from the landscape can actually strengthen our connection to it. And, if sited appropriately, an aerial tramway is a fine transit system to foster that connection.

CHICAGO

The El (or L) provides an interesting and positively unintentional footnote to the social opportunity of transit. Many of the laudable design elements that are found in the circulators of Seattle, San Francisco, and Santa Barbara are not present in Chicago's, yielding a rather banal passenger experience. However, it is not the circulators themselves that are the most disappointing but rather the system's defining feature: the elevated tracks. While the passenger experience may be quite ordinary, the experience for the pedestrian below is extraordinarily unpleasant.

Within the downtown core, the elevated steel tracks block sightlines down the otherwise nicely detailed streets of "The Loop." The tracks are wholly utilitarian in design and, hence, not particularly pleasant to look at. They are wide and low-slung and constructed with a clutter of steel-bracing and cross-supports, much of which is covered in rust, soot, and guano and topped with a chaotic assemblage of diminutive and haphazardly fitted platform stations that look more like products of shanty-towns than Chi-town. The elevated tracks, as one passing pedestrian remarked, are "about as ugly a rail line that one could design."[7]

For comparison, the steel tracks' form and construction lack the elegance and airiness of the concrete superstructure built for Seattle's monorail. Such airiness is imperative for sidewalk comfort, as skylight is always a precious commodity in a city of skyscrapers. As one might surmise, the streets that the El runs above are considerably darker and visually harsher than other streets in the Loop. Many of downtown Chicago's streets—Lake, Wabash, and Wells, for example—have all the makings of stately, urbane people-places. These streets are lined with elegant storefronts, many with eye-pleasing, two-story window displays. Buildings designed by architects of international renown punctuate the street corners. Honey locust trees, flower pots, and decorative light standards define what could be an active and pleasing pedestrian realm along broad sidewalks. But for those damn elevated tracks! They seem to suck all the light—and life—from the sidewalks below.

The elevated tracks also hide many of Chicago's notable architectural features. One instance is the Chicago Theatre's iconic blade sign and marquee, a photogenic and highly sought-after landmark for visitors. The theater is located at the intersection of State and Lake streets, just one block south of the Chicago River. Few landmarks could effectively compete for the attention of pedestrians ogling the emerald green waterway, but the Chicago Theatre might be effective, if given the chance. Its sign and marquee certainly command one's attention and rightfully so, but the breadth, height, and design of the elevated tracks running along Lake Street veil this beautifully renovated historical land-mark, and it is often bypassed by passersby.

Sight is not the only physiological sense that is assaulted. A person cannot be alone with his or her thoughts, let alone converse with another, when a train passes overhead. The sound that emanates above—steel wheels on steel rails reverberating through steel columns and beams, all the while bouncing off stone and concrete building facades—is a sharp noise that tends toward a shrill, piercing, ear-splitting unpleasantness. The elevated tracks also create psychological barriers to pedestrian through-movement. When one encounters an intersection with Lake, Wells, Van Buren, or Wabash, the tracks of the El loom overhead, casting dark shadows below, conveying an ominous message of "pass through at your own risk," for it is often hard to see the vehicular traffic. The aural, visual, and psychological unpleasantness found along these streets is a deterrent to pedestrian activity, and it is a relief to turn the corner and finally be out of earshot, and eyesight, of the El.

Though the experience for pedestrians would be greatly improved along Chicago's downtown streets with quieter conditions, better sight-lines, and more light reaching the sidewalks, it would be difficult to mount a strong argument for a complete redesign of the transit system. Since it began service in 1892, the El has become a fixture within Chicago, attaining iconic status. In a 2005 poll conducted by *The Chicago Tribune*, readers nominated the El as one of Chicago's "Seven Wonders." Obviously, the El is an incredible source of pride for Chicagoans, as even the Chicago River did not make the list. In the final voting, the El bested even the more internationally famous Chicago icon, the Sears Tower.[8] Of course, the longevity and necessity of the El commands citizen respect, though it is more likely that an outsider will never appreciate the system as Chicagoans do. For visitors, it is not so much a beloved and wondrous architectural creation as it is more mundanely a necessary and tolerable engineering endeavor. But its absence would certainly leave a hole in the Loop and forever change the city's image, for both residents and visitors.

TOP: THE EL'S INFRASTRUCTURE SCARES LIFE AWAY FROM THE OTHERWISE PEOPLE-FRIENDLY STREETS.

BOTTOM: COLORED SIGNS AND COLORED BANDS ON STATION POLES ATTEMPT TO CLARIFY THE SEVEN COLOR-CODED ROUTES THAT SUFFUSE THE LOOP ON THE MAP.

In addition to the lamentable design characteristics of the overhead tracks, the routes themselves are somewhat problematic for the El's riders. Seven color-coded routes circulate through the downtown core, often puzzling even the most seasoned transit users. Pink, red, orange, purple, brown, blue, and green lines produce a kaleidoscope of train routes that are often difficult to distinguish, even with sharp eyes. Distinguishing the routes with certainty is hampered by the condition of the transit maps hanging on the walls of each station; many of the maps are old, weathered, and even defaced. For reasons unbeknownst even to station operators, some of the transit maps are mounted below waist level, with the enlarged "Downtown Detail" depicted toward the bottom. This requires that one squat deeply or get on all fours to read the map effectively.

To say that downtown Chicago's Technicolor transit map produces some confusion is certainly an understatement. Yet this serendipitously leads to friendly discussion between passengers, both on the platforms and in the transit cars. It seems that the most common topic of conversation between riders is the perplexity of Chicago's transit system. The somewhat casual arrangement of seating within the train cars easily allow passengers in distress to ask assistance of those who appear to have solved the transit map mystery. Strangers who have been in the same predicament once upon a time freely exhibit patience and offer explanation of the train route conundrums.

It is dubious to argue for designing perplexity into transit systems for the sake of social opportunity. Perplexity is certainly not something Chicago wants to promote, as the Chicago Transit Authority has worked diligently over years past on graphics that better clarify the puzzling color-coded routes depicted on maps of the Loop. Platforms now have colored bands painted on poles to help relieve uncertainty as to what trains pass through. In spite of these attempts, the routes are still problematic, and it is interesting how the confusion felt among so many passengers of Chicago's transit leads to conversation between strangers. The riddling routes seem to serve as a communication icebreaker of sorts, a commonality that encourages passengers to greet strangers and ask for assistance. Sometimes, if the ride is long enough, the conversation extends beyond the mere explanation of the "El's" nuances onto other topics about Chicago. Regardless of the topic of conversation, it is uplifting to hear strangers offer assistance to those in need. Big cities typically breed anonymity. Within these environs, we are not compelled to offer assistance, because we are often busy avoiding eye contact.

On a warm, summer weekday, waiting on a platform for an Orange Line train, a young woman of Jewish descent asked an elderly African-American woman a question about the Purple Line. The elderly woman, unsure of the answer, in turn asked an Asian tourist if he knew the answer. The tourist, possessing a guidebook, quickly found a legible transit route map and, with help from the other two persons, was able to send the young woman in the correct direction. Onboard the Orange Line train, a Hispanic mother and her daughter were trying to decipher the transit map, when a young Caucasian man offered his assistance. The Hispanic mother could not speak English, though her daughter could, with slight difficulty. The young man patiently explained the transit route, so the young woman could at once comprehend the system while translating the directions to her mother. Meanwhile, a middle-aged African-American couple discussed how to get to a certain train station with a middle-aged Caucasian woman. After a lengthy conversation that included more than Chicago's transit, the couple stood up to off-board and offered gratitude and pleasantries to the helpful stranger.

For some, these may seem like trivial acts of kindness in a magnificently diverse city. But that short train ride offered promise of a ubiquitous social harmony that we dare dream is imminent.

THE VIVID "PETER WITT" TRAMS ARE PERENNIAL CROWD-PLEASERS IN SAN FRANCISCO.

"Bus lines would be a good deal less expensive. But against this saving should be weighted, first, passenger comfort which has some money value even if it cannot be demonstrated, and second, the market value of an institution which helps make the city stand out among cities of the world."

—EDITORIAL IN *THE SAN FRANCISCO CHRONICLE*, FEBRUARY 3, 1947.

Shortly after World War II, Americans essentially lost the knack for creating comfortable and joyful city streets and public spaces. Comfort and joy disappeared from our public transit systems as well. A utilitarian, "no frills" ethic dominated public transit design, yielding vehicles nobody wanted to ride unless they absolutely had to. Passenger consideration in public transit design became a low priority, as the nation was clearly headed toward a land of private mobility centered on the automobile and truck. The morphology of our towns and cities changed dramatically, and automobile design reached its apogee. Automotive makers excelled in providing stylized, comfortable machines with heart-fluttering appeal and visceral thrill. For society in the mid-twentieth century, it was easy to leave the public vehicle for a private one.

Although America has been infatuated with the automobile ever since, there is growing concern about and resentment toward the automobile today. The loss of personal and family time due to interminable commutes and traffic congestion; the environmental damage and loss of natural habitat linked to sprawl; the rising costs of gasoline, maintenance, and insurance for the private citizen; the frightening increase in costs for highway maintenance and a deteriorating infrastrutcture; and the erosion of our sense of place and community—these and other factors are renewing the interest in public transportation among planners, developers, politicians, and passengers alike. As the esteemed geographer Cotton Mather noted, most presciently, "We have only begun to deal with the automobile—both in America and, increasingly, the world."[1]

Banal public vehicles are not the answer to our public transportation needs, and it might behoove us to take a page from the design manual for private automobiles. To guarantee the popularity of transit in this nation once again, these public vehicles will have to possess the style, comfort, heart-fluttering appeal, and visceral thrill of private automobiles and more. A ride aboard transit should be seen as an opportunity to connect with all kinds of people and all kinds of places within a city, a compelling offer that the automobile cannot match. Quite simply, people should *want* to ride public vehicles, not feel as if they have to.

We must begin to think about public transit as a purveyor of community. Like all public space, the transit car is neutral territory, in which demographic restrictions are necessarily—and refreshingly—absent. Places where people can go and see strangers as well as regulars are settings for community, and the transit car eminently qualifies as such a place. By recognizing the transit car as public space, it becomes evident that we must ensure that the design of public transportation is conducive to public life. To accomplish this, transit car design needs to "fit" with our predisposed human conditions, providing physical and psychological comfort. The whole of the transit system should allow us to become better connected to our community by easily allowing us to survey and appreciate the landscape and built environment of our home place and by facilitating conversation and social engagement with our community brethren.

Toward these goals, the remaining pages outline essential design considerations for those dimensions of public transportation that can enrich our passenger experience and provide the settings for community life that many of us long for. These dimensions provide a checklist of sorts, to help ensure sufficient thought has been given to such questions as: What form will the transit system take? What route does it travel? How often does it come by? What is its power source? What is the traveling speed? Who operates the transit vehicle, if anyone? Other, more detailed decisions have to be made regarding the circulator itself, such as the size and style of the transit car, the quality, orientation and fenestration of seating and its relationship to those both seated and standing, the type of materials inside the cabin and out, its color, its heating/cooling, and its lighting. To give consideration to only one or two of these dimensions is insufficient. Public transportation that is highly valued by a city's citizens and its visitors, whether they ride it or not, exhibits attention to many, if not all, of these dimensions. As such, it is difficult to rank the importance of one dimension over another; they are all important.

The following design considerations for public transportation in America are offered (on pages 126–56) in no hierarchal sequence other than to begin with the larger planning considerations, progress to the fussy design details, and conclude with the more intangible, philosophical concerns that promote vitality, community, and prosperity.

THE LAS VEGAS MONORAIL SNAKES AROUND UTILITY POLES, PARKING RAMPS, GARAGES, STORAGE FACILITIES, AND MAINTENANCE SHEDS RATHER THAN ALONG OR BESIDE THE FAMOUS LAS VEGAS STRIP. THUS, THE ROUTE AFFORDS A UTILITARIAN PANORAMA THAT IS ENTIRELY FORGETTABLE.

THE ROUTE

In his attentive book, *The Experience of Place*, Tony Hiss reminds us, "People are often drawn to places that offer rich experiences: beautiful landscapes, glittering theater districts, tranquil neighborhoods."[2] The environment through which the transit car passes—its route—is an important consideration for providing access to those places that offer rich passenger experiences. Transit route planning often follows the dictum that a straight line provides the shortest distance between two destinations, thus presenting the logical path of travel.

The most efficient route, however, may not be the most pleasurable one. The San Francisco cable car is a good case in point. What makes the cable car routes so memorable and attractive are the number of city "jewels" it serves. The Powell-Mason line, as an example, begins at Powell and Market streets, travels along Powell for almost a mile before it turns west for one block, finishing its journey along Mason Street. Along that Powell Street mile, the cable car passes Union Square and the downtown shopping district, the stately St. Francis hotel, the Sir Francis Drake hotel with its doormen in full beefeater regalia, Chinatown, and other notable landmarks. The distance separating Mason from Powell is only 412 feet, short enough that, if transit planners would design the route today, they might consider, Why not run the route straight up and down Mason? Why go through the expense of adding extra pulleys, cable, tracks, and switches for one block? If the cable car did not run on Powell Street, as it currently does, but went along a more direct route straight up Mason Street, the richness of the experience would be lost. Mason Street between Market and Jackson simply does not provide the eye-catching, heart-fluttering appeal that Powell Street possesses, a mere 412 feet away.

Obviously, San Francisco is unique. What of those countless other town and city streets that, like Mason, do not possess the appeal of a Powell Street? Does the entire route have to be eye-catching? It certainly helps, and that should be the goal. San Francisco aside, transit route planning must start with the realization that, in every city and in every neighborhood, regardless of its current state of prosperity, some streets have better architecture along them than others; some offer finer views of the landscape; some have more people on them and, thus, more activity; some have cultural venues and civic opportunities; some have landmarks; some have enhanced landscaping; and some even offer savory smells and lively sounds. These are just modest characteristics of a potential transit route that provide interest to passengers. Conversely, streets composed predominantly of gas stations, used car dealerships, parking lots, and strip malls make for dull transit routes, though they may yield less travel time for passengers to their ultimate destination. People are usually willing to forego a few minutes in overall transit time if it means they will be justly compensated with a delightful ride. Efficiency—the shortest distance between two destinations—should not be the principal determinant for transit route planning. Rather, passenger experience—those spaces and places that provide the most interest—should be the driver.

FORM

Among the first questions a municipality needs to ask when considering public transportation are: What form shall the transit system take? Should it be a bus or a shuttle? A futuristic monorail or a historic streetcar? Most transportation engineers give priority to those systems that

EVEN THOUGH THE TECHNOLOGY IS WELL OVER A CENTURY OLD, FUNICULARS (SUCH AS THIS ONE IN DUBUQUE, IOWA) STILL PROVIDE AN EFFICIENT MEANS OF TRAVERSING PRECIPITOUS SLOPES. THE VISCERAL THRILL INHERENT WITH THIS FORM OF TRANSPORTATION ENSURES POPULARITY WITH PASSENGERS.

move the largest number of people as quickly as possible for the least amount of capital cost. While efficiency and economics are certainly key considerations, transportation decision-makers should also consider the passenger's desires. The decision to run transit below ground, above ground, or at grade should be guided by a philosophy of delight. Whether it is a sleek, multi-car monorail train that glides over city streets or a slow-rolling, chuggin' streetcar that eases its way through them, transit should respond to its setting in a way that delights both passengers and onlookers.

Delight is often based on the appropriateness of the transit system within the setting it travels. The form of transit that best reflects the city's urban context—both geographical and historical   is one that not only provides captivating experiences, but is often highly valued by the public. The sleek, modern monorail in Seattle is a good fit within the urban context of the sleek, modern high-rises of downtown. Its futuristic form reflects such futuristic architecture as the Space Needle and Frank Gehry's building for the Experience Music Project, both found along the monorail's route. Though it was intended merely as an ephemeral experiment in public transportation, the delight it brings citizens and visitors has given longevity to this form of transit.

San Francisco's cable car is an appropriate form of transit, given the undulating geography of the city. "Its perpetuation is an argument for logic, not for nostalgia," notes historian Christopher Swan. "Despite the system's status as a national landmark and the often overzealous attention of tourists and traditionalists, the cable railroad remains a practical means of transportation for San Francisco."[3] Much of the cable car's appeal is its seemingly miraculous, effortless ascent up and over the precipitous faces of Nob Hill and Russian Hill. There is reason for the cable car's existence. Conversely, a cable car ride on pancake-flat terrain would certainly have diminished appeal. To merely copy its form without consideration of its geographical context is short-sighted. The long-term value would certainly depreciate.

Historical context is another important consideration in determining the form of transit. The reincarnation of a historical streetcar, for example, gives insight into how our parents and grandparents moved about the city. The streetcar gave form and a particular order to cities, requiring the built environment to be compact, scaled to the slower pace of the pedestrian. Automobiles and buses do not yield clues to the origins of our older cities but streetcars can. They help provide legibility to the development and redevelopment of our downtowns and city centers. This added meaning is enriching and can increase value to our urban transport systems while enhancing our experience aboard them.

SCALE

Intimacy is compelling, and transit vehicles should err on the small side rather than the large. The cabin's interior should be scaled to the passenger, and the overall size of the vehicle should be scaled to the pedestrian. It is understandable, for reasons of economics and efficiency, to utilize the largest vehicles that can adequately fit on the street. As vehicle size increases, however, policing becomes more difficult, especially toward the rear. More importantly, lengthy passenger carriers exhibit difficulty negotiating corners. We've all stood at the corner waiting to cross the street, while witnessing a large bus making a right turn. Frequently, the rear tires ride up on the curb, forcing pedestrians to take a few steps back. To solve this problem, engineers design generous curb radii to facilitate these vehicles in their turning maneuvers rather than use smaller transit vehicles. This increase in street-corner radius necessarily comes at the expense of the pedestrian realm. Sidewalks are whittled away at the corners, increasing the distances pedestrians have to walk to cross the street. Furthermore, a large curb radius facilitates not only bus maneuvers, but those of private automobiles as well. Drivers can effectively negotiate a corner with a large radius without having to brake, potentially resulting in perilous condi-

DISNEYLAND'S OMNIBUS DOUBLES PASSENGER CAPACITY BY STACKING TWO INTIMATELY SCALED CABINS RATHER THAN PROVIDING ONE LONG CABIN. THIS ARRANGEMENT MAINTAINS A PEDESTRIAN SCALE BEFITTING MAIN STREET, U.S.A.

tions for the pedestrian. Confoundedly, planning for longer transit vehicles can actually be in direct *opposition* to planning for walkable, pedestrian-friendly streets.

There are at least two solutions to the problem of designing intimately scaled transit vehicles while also providing for larger passenger capacity. Increasing the interval frequency of the transit cars, or headway, provides one answer (more on that later). Another solution, common to cities outside the United States, such as London and Hong Kong, effortlessly solves the problem of transit car size versus passenger capacity by utilizing two cabins stacked atop each other. Double-decker buses and trams, highly sought after by tourists as well as commuters, provide single operators twice the passenger capacity while offering two intimately

AS THESE SAN FRANCISCO STREET CARS EXEMPLIFY, THE USE OF SMALLER TRANSIT VEHICLES THAT COME BY MORE FREQUENTLY ENLIVENS THE STREET SCENE FOR PEDESTRIANS WHILE PROVIDING CONVENIENCE TO PASSENGERS.

scaled interiors, each with their own distinctive passenger perspectives and experiences. Another benefit of double-decker transit car design is that such vehicles tend to dominate the animation along the street, as they tower over adjacent automobiles, pickup trucks, and even SUVs. Increased visibility of public transportation reminds pedestrians of their choices in mobility, and the likelihood they will choose public transit over their private automobile often increases as well.[4]

HEADWAY

Headway is the length of time between two transit vehicles for any given route. Similar to form and scale, the headway of transit vehicles also faces concerns over cost. In general, one large vehicle that comes every thirty minutes is more economical to operate than three smaller vehicles that come every ten minutes. Obviously, a balance between headway and operating costs is needed. The frustration one feels from narrowly missing the bus or train and having to wait thirty minutes for the next one is enough for many to shun public transit altogether. This is especially true in geographic regions with extreme climates. In Davenport, Iowa, where summer temperatures can surpass ninety degrees and winter often sees days in the single digits, buses on many routes run but once each hour, even during the morning and evening commute. It is little wonder that there is a paucity of transit passengers in this city. Public transportation with shorter headways offers many benefits to potential passengers, most notably convenience. Freedom from a schedule is one of our biggest attractions to the automobile. Even if the overall journey is more expensive and takes longer in our cars, the ability to leave anytime we want, without wait, is enticing.[5]

Shorter headway times offer more than convenience, however. A higher frequency of transit vehicles provides a helpful reminder of our transportation options. Buses on some city streets in Davenport, for example, are rare sightings, largely because they only come through once per hour, so many residents are unaware that public transit even exists for their neighborhood. Out of sight, out of mind.

A higher frequency of transit vehicles better creates an original animated scene along the route it travels. A splendid example of this can be witnessed on Market Street in San Francisco. Different colored streetcars with various styles can be seen two, sometimes three, in a bunch, suffusing the street with a rainbow of color. Perhaps the best place to capture transit-animated streets in this city is along the cable car routes. On Powell Street, it is a treat to see three cars spaced relatively close together, ascending Nob Hill while one or two are traveling back down in the opposite direction. The beguiling animation found along Market and Powell streets is largely the result of public

IT IS ONLY FITTING THAT A NATURAL ENVIRONMENT AND SETTING AS BREATHTAKING AS SANTA
BARBARA'S HAS A TRANSIT VEHICLE OPERATED BY A CLEAN-AIR POWER SOURCE. IT WOULD BE AN
ENVIRONMENTAL INDIGNITY IF THIS SHUTTLE WERE TO RUMBLE ASIDE THE CITY'S SERENE, PARA-
DISIACAL BEACHES, EXPELLING CLOUDS OF DIESEL EXHAUST ALONG THE WAY.

transportation. For many, public transit defines these streets. Powell
Street *is* the cable car line. Market Street *is* the F-line, even though
automobile traffic is greater. The frequency of transit vehicles passing
through these streets colors our memory of them.

OPERATION

Transit is increasingly becoming more mechanized and automated,
and this is unfortunate. Transit operators can provide a feeling of
comfort and security. Operators answer questions, help keep order
within the vehicle, and are welcome, familiar faces to regular passengers. On some systems, operators can make change, making transit
more convenient as "exact fare" eludes us one time or another. Fare

boxes that require exact change, prerecorded voices announcing transit stops, seats that are located too far from the driver to facilitate small talk, or signs forbidding conversation altogether—these are just a few seemingly benign details of transit systems today that contribute to a more robotic, less human feel. Driverless forms of transit—often the most asocial—do not provide the approachable, authoritative figure to whom questions can be addressed or delinquent behavior policed. As a substitute in Las Vegas, pre-recorded information is piped into each of the passenger cabins within the monorail. This continuously looping information is a bit distracting and quickly becomes annoying. People like to hear friendly voices but more so from live humans. Human operators add color and flair to a transit vehicle.

It is important not only to consider *who* operates the transit vehicles, but *how* they are operated as well. The most memorable transit systems often employ the most unique sources of locomotion. The horses that pull streetcars on rails through Main Street in Disneyland remain perennial favorites among children and adults alike. Assumedly, humans will always be drawn to animals, as they have an uncanny ability to provoke wonderment. The cables, cogs, and drums that pull funiculars up the faces of Pittsburgh's river bluffs are fascinating and are on display for curious onlookers. Chattanooga and Santa Barbara both eschewed gasoline as a power source and made an ecological statement with electric-powered shuttles, a statement lauded by residents as well as tourists. It will be interesting to see how the public embraces New York City's ensuing fleet of hybrid taxicabs. Assumedly, Mayor Bloomberg's mandate will prove immensely popular with the city's citizens. People today increasingly yearn for more "green" experiences and ways to lighten their ecological imprint. Not only is the air cleaner with electric and hybrid-powered vehicles, but streets are quieter and passenger cabins are more conducive to conversation.

SAN FRANCISCO'S CABLE CARS TRAVEL AT A MODEST NINE-MILES-PER-HOUR PACE, BARELY
FASTER THAN A JOGGER, WHICH ALLOWS EVEN THE ELDERLY TO SAFELY ENJOY AN EXHILARATING
RIDE ON THE RUNNING BOARDS.

PACE

Transit vehicles, like the streets they run on, are complex settings that can
host a variety of activities. Speed and efficiency, though important considerations, should not be the sole criteria for successful transit, just as
streets should not be designed exclusively for these purposes either. This
logic is what turned our once-vibrant city streets into nothing more than
conduits for fast automobile travel. Pedestrian life ceased, businesses
suffered, and the overall quality of the street declined. Likewise, designing
the transit car and transit route for the single purpose of moving people
as quickly as possible through the city yields a diminished experience for
both the passenger inside the vehicle and the pedestrian along the street.
A passenger vehicle that travels a mere ten miles per hour, such as the

New Orleans's streetcar, may be anathema to current transportation ideology. Indeed, such a pace, modestly more brisk than jogging, requires all traffic to move with leisure. Time that is lost to the destination, however, is time afforded to the passenger to people-watch, window-shop, and sightsee, to take pleasure in the sounds and voices heard along the street, and to savor the aromas of cafés, bakeries, blossoms, and unique scents of a place. A slow-moving vehicle adds welcome animation to the street, drawing people to it, unlike a fast one from which safety-minded pedestrians keep their distance.

STYLE

Style, for the purposes of this book, is the transit car's interior and exterior detailing, the impression of overall form and character conveyed through its individual, distinctive features. Attention to style is

THIS BOAT TRAM (PART OF SAN FRANCISCO'S QUIRKY AND DIVERSE "F-LINE" FLEET) EXHIBITS A STYLE WHOLLY CONGRUENT WITH THE MARITIME ENVIRONMENT ALONG THE EMBARCADERO.

necessary to provide a valued, memorable transit experience. Style can evoke feelings of nostalgia (e.g., streetcars), which itself can be compelling. Style can reinforce the overall architectural language along a particular transit route (e.g., the Victorian-styled cable cars of San Francisco) or stand in stark contrast to it. Style can reflect the history, culture, or technological aptitude of a city at a particular time (e.g., Seattle's monorail built for the 1962 World's Fair), either past or present. Style can play many roles in public transportation's ability to entice pedestrians to board.

Shuttles provide an excellent form of transportation for articulating the importance of style. A good comparison is the style of Santa Barbara's shuttle vis-à-vis the one used in Phoenix. The Santa Barbara shuttle exhibits a style similar to an open-air, canvas-canopied tram, such as those commonly found in zoos and amusement parks. It is a simple style but long on charm. Phoenix's shuttle, on the other hand, basically looks like (and is) a shortened bus. Its copper color is but one component of style—a delightful one—but the overall style of the Phoenix shuttle lacks the panache of Santa Barbara's.

A popular trend in transit design today is to outfit shuttles in a style that mimics vintage streetcars. These streetcar-styled shuttles are popping up in large and small cities throughout America. Originally, they were aimed at tourists, used principally for sightseeing. Increasingly, municipalities, such as Staunton, Virginia, are also using them for public transit, often dubbing them "historic trolleys." They certainly add a bit whimsy and character along urban streets, and they can be eye-catching. But one questions the long-term value of a transit style—or any style—that lacks authenticity and meaning.

Streetcars used quiet, clean electricity for their power source, and the overhead tangle of wires was part of their charm. They ran on smooth, steel rails. Many streetcars did not have windows, providing an open-air cabin. If windows were fitted, they were completely clear and operable. The streetcars of yore also exhibited exquisite attention to architectural detail and ornament. These details are important components of the overall style of the streetcar, components that compel passengers and solicit lasting value. Shuttles that are merely styled after vintage streetcars, however, often lack these compelling components. These shuttles typically use a diesel engine for propulsion. There is no additional infrastructure other than asphalt roads, which are often uneven and pot-holed, providing a ride that lacks the smoothness of rails. The cabin's windows are often heavily tinted and sealed. Decals take the place of real architectural details. While true streetcars often gave reason to a city's form and existence, necessitating a network of human-scaled, pedestrian-friendly streets, some cities that employ these "historic trolleys" never even had a streetcar system, nor would the urban fabric logically support one. Though there is an initial cuteness to this type of transit car, it is difficult to imagine the false fronts providing fond and lasting memories.

The transit vehicle's interior style and detailing is just as important as for the exterior. An appropriate exterior style catches our eyes and beckons us aboard. The inside helps determine whether we enjoy our journey or are anxious to flee. Transit car cabins can be detailed to create an ambiance of tranquility and warmth or one of sterility. Here, materials and craftsmanship are instrumental in creating the desired style. Tampa's streetcars and their judicious use of polished wood and brass, with accents of leather and soft incandescent lighting overhead, recall a style reminiscent of an old New England bar. Transit cars that incorporate materials commonly found in newer systems today, such as bright fluorescent lights, molded plastic seats and paneling, and linoleum-tiled floors, seem to take their styling cues from the interiors of fast-food restaurants. It is obvious which style welcomes riders to linger and which urges them out the door.

LOOKING OUT A PARTIALLY OPEN WINDOW ABOARD A SHUTTLE IN UTAH'S ZION NATIONAL PARK, THE DELETERIOUS EFFECTS OF TINTING WINDOWS BECOME CLEAR. TINTED WINDOWS MUTE VIVID PANORAMAS, YIELDING A DULL PASSENGER EXPERIENCE.

TRANSPARENCY

Glare can be a problem for passengers, designers of transit cars will argue, and windows with a dark tint are, thus, deemed necessary for a passenger's comfort. Seldom does one find a transit vehicle today without tinted windows, some so heavily shaded that nobody on the outside can see in. Besides, tinted windows provide for sleek, contemporary designs that appeal to passengers, right? While glare may be a problem for some people, and even then only during the early morning or late afternoon, tinted windows do not provide the best opportunity for passenger enrichment. City streets are filled with color and light, and shading this vibrancy with tinted windows dulls our experiences. Many streetcar systems solve the problem of glare, simply and elegantly, by providing an operable shade that can be pulled down over the completely transparent window. Passengers who want to reduce glare may use the shade, while other riders who wish to look out onto the city's unadulterated kaleidoscope of color can leave the shade up.

Clear windows also reduce the need for artificial light within the cabin. Some transit vehicles have such heavily tinted windows that it becomes necessary to have interior fluorescent lights on throughout the day. People respond positively to natural light. It's easy on our eyes and gives us comfort. Seattle's monorail is designed with an abundance of clear windows that run along the sides and the roof of the train, bathing the cabin in natural light. The monorail's windows are so generous in both size and frequency that even people who have to stand are rewarded with visual comfort and fantastic views.

This brings up another important consideration in transit car design. Most often windows are sized and placed solely for the seated passenger, yet our most successful transit systems are often packed with standees. Offering up one's seat to another who could benefit more is certainly a commendable, civil gesture. Such a gesture should not be punished with a restricted view. Standees should be offered the same views granted to those seated.

A window's operability is another important feature in achieving transparency. Sealed windows seem to be standard issue for public transportation today. In some cases, windows with small vents, located high above the passenger's head over the main windows, allow a modicum of permeability. But the small size of the vent glass, its location atop the main window, its restricted operability, and the fact that it is tinted as well do little to achieve cabin transparency, other than allowing modest air circulation. Certainly, there are times when windows should be kept closed, usually because of inclement weather. But, during periods of brilliant days and nights, which every city experiences

THE SEATING ARRANGEMENT WITHIN SEATTLE'S MONORAIL PROVIDES CHOICES IN ORIENTATION. PASSENGERS MAY CHOOSE TO FACE FORWARD, BACKWARD, OR TO THE SIDE, WHERE THEY ARE AFFORDED BETTER VIEWS OF THE PASSING LANDSCAPE. THERE ARE EVEN SEATS NEXT TO THE TRAIN OPERATOR, FAVORITES AMONG CHILDREN AND ADULTS ALIKE.

regardless of geography, passengers should be allowed access to fresh air. An open window allows passengers to connect better with a place by engaging their physiological senses. Open windows naturally allow better views of street scenes and of pedestrian faces; they also permit unfiltered natural light to enter the cabin. An open window allows one to hear the sounds of the city, perhaps even to interact vocally with pedestrians. City scents—such as those naturally present in marine, prairie, desert, or alpine air; nature in bloom; the aromas of cafés or eateries; or even those smells that are not so pleasant—are allowed unobstructed access through an open window and can greatly enrich the passenger experience. Our sense of touch is also important, and passengers should be able feel the warmth of the sun on their arm or a cool breeze across their face. Just as a convertible provides a more stimulating ride than the same model automobile with a hardtop, a transparent passenger cabin can dramatically transform the environs of the transit car from a stifled and sealed setting into one that is inviting and engaging.

SEATING

Choice in seating, specifically with regard to its location and orientation, is one of the most important and, seemingly, overlooked considerations in enjoyable transit design. Properly composed seating, like that of a great park or plaza, can be the single greatest component of successful transit. The composition of seating, or grouping of seats, should provide for a variety of gathering opportunities. The best transit cars provide solitary seats for passengers preferring to be alone, paired seats that are desirable for couples, and two sets of paired seats, oriented toward each other, that are desirable for a larger group interested in conversing during the trip. Seating can be *sociopetal*; that is, arranged inward in a manner that encourages eye contact and small talk with others (e.g., the shuttles employed in Santa Barbara and Chattanooga). Or seating can be *sociofugal*; that is, oriented outward to facilitate views of the passing scene (e.g., the end cabins within San Francisco's cable cars). The best views are generally up front, next to the driver. It seems transit everywhere can take a cue from Seattle's monorail and allow a lucky passenger or two the opportunity to ride shotgun.

It seems a worthwhile endeavor to incorporate seating in which the passenger has a modicum of control over orientation and which can heighten enjoyment. The St. Charles streetcar in New Orleans offers some control in orientation by allowing passengers to flip the backrest of the wooden seats from one side to the other. Perhaps something more can be employed. Curiously, seats that swivel, which provide a variety of orientation opportunities for passengers, are categorically absent from public transit, a situation worthy of exploration.

Another important consideration for seating, one also often overlooked, is an arrangement allowing passengers ample space to stand, if they choose to. The best transit systems not only provide comfortable standing areas, but reward standees with an experience that is different and sometimes better than if they were seated. Arguably, the most exhilarating space a passenger can claim on the cable car is the running board, designated for standees only. Similarly, San Francisco's Milan streetcars provide ample room for standees at the rear of the passenger cabin, where views are far superior to those seen when seated. The Roosevelt Island Tramway in New York City is comprised almost entirely of standing room and, thus, offers an infinite number of passenger gathering arrangements, regardless of group size.

COLOR

Color adds fancy and can give transit vehicles distinction. At one time in our nation's transit history, color was dependent upon place. Cities dressed their streetcars in unique liveries, giving the cars—and the cities—identity. Streetcars in Los Angeles were two-tone yellow, fitting for this sunlit city; Louisville's cars were green and cream; and Baltimore's were yellow with a gray roof, Kansas City's cream and black, and San Francisco's blue and gold. Slowly, the brightly colored vehicles that once punctuated our city streets were muted, replaced with vehicles dressed the same, regardless of location.

Color can be the saving grace for an otherwise banal transit vehicle. One can argue that the most redeemable characteristic of Phoenix's downtown circulator is its color. The copper-clad shuttle strengthens the identity of Copper Square, while providing much needed animation to the downtown district's streets. The shuttle's cop-

"TAXI-CAB YELLOW" IS THE DOMINANT COLOR OF VEHICLES—AND TULIPS—ALONG PARK AVENUE IN MIDTOWN MANHATTAN.

per dress is what helps connect the passenger to place and has the strongest potential of leaving any lasting impression.

The chosen colors for the transit vehicle may be harmonious within the landscape it travels. The olive-green of the St. Charles streetcar, for example, is a natural, fitting hue for the tree-lined streets of New Orleans's Garden District. Santa Barbara's stark-white shuttle with sea-green trim is wholly appropriate for this seaside community. It looks to be a product of the ocean, a gleaming shell found along the beach. The color of transit can also stand in stark contrast to its setting. Nowhere is such a contrast in color more welcome than on the streets of New York City, where taxis create rivulets of yellow that flow through the gray canyon walls of Manhattan. Color adds vitality and international recognition, giving transit iconic status and a source of civic pride.

INCANDESCENT BULBS ENSHROUDED IN ORNAMENTAL GLASS REFRACTORS PROVIDE ELEGANT TOUCHES OF HOME INSIDE THE CABIN OF THIS PETER WITT TRAM IN SAN FRANCISCO. THE DESIGN OF ONE GLASS REFRACTOR OFTEN DIFFERS SLIGHTLY FROM THE OTHERS, ADDING TO THESE TRAMS' QUIRKY CHARM.

LIGHTING

Comfort, safety, and appeal are paramount to transit popularity, and the single most important physical characteristic after the sun sets is lighting. A vibrant city is a continuum of day and night. The myriad bars and clubs, theaters and entertainment venues, late-night bookstores and cafés are attractive to a diverse and abundant population that may rely on transit to and from these social gathering spots. People are loath to enter any public space, transit car or otherwise, if they feel security has been compromised. Proper lighting goes a long way in not only ensuring peace of mind, but in contributing energy and animation to a city scene. The best transit vehicles use warm, soft incandescent lighting within their cabins versus the sterile florescent lighting common within city buses. The streetcars in San Francisco and New Orleans provide great examples of comfortable glows of luminescence that seem to bathe their interiors in light rather than bleach them. Mood is important in the enjoyment of any space, and lighting can have a great effect. The ambiance commonly found in romantic restaurants, however, may be a bit dim for the transit car. Thus, a balance between safety and comfort, efficacy and color rendition must be struck. Good lighting ensures that one can see adequately into the passenger cabin and out as well. Passengers should be able to window-shop during their commute home and not have the windows return reflections of themselves and other passengers.

CONNECTION TO PLACE

Human creations borne of challenges unique to a place have special significance. It is, perhaps, why citizens of Pittsburgh have such an affinity for bridges, for example, as their lives circumnavigate the city's three rivers. Memorable transit is unique to a place and the people it serves, and it should respond to the special qualities inherent to that place. These responses can be environmental, such as the funicular's relationship to the bluffs that define Pittsburgh's river valley or the beach-appropriate, open-air shuttle's relationship to Santa Barbara's climate. Responses may be historical: the monorail of the 1962 World's Fair provides an important piece to Seattle's history, as it exemplifies the city's aspirations at the time. Or transit can respond to the culture of place, which is effectively demonstrated by Portland's transit route 63, along which a brightly painted bus known as "ART" shuttles passengers between the city's numerous museums, gardens, and performance venues. Public transportation vehicles may even reflect the predominant architectural language of the city, such

CHATTANOOGA'S LOOKOUT MOUNTAIN INCLINE RAILWAY OFFERS A VISUAL AND VISCERAL MEANS TO EXPERIENCE THIS HISTORIC LANDSCAPE, SITE OF A SIGNIFICANT CIVIL WAR BATTLE IN NOVEMBER 1863 THAT "SEALED THE FATE OF THE CONFEDERACY."

as the Victorian-styled cable cars of San Francisco. Other transit details, such as fenestration and a carefully planned route, can offer passengers expansive views of the passing landscape, strengthening their understanding of the surrounding geography.

Place can provide the raison d'être for a particular transit system, such as the Roosevelt Island's aerial tram. Or transit can instruct the order and form of place, such as the streetcar. A one-size-fits-all ideology, which seems to predominate with bus design, may not be the most conducive to creating memorable transit by strengthening our connection to place. Connection to place begins by examining how the form of transit, the design details of the transit car, and the transit route all contribute to our experience of the geography of place, the culture of place, the history of place, and the aspirations of that place.

CASUAL AND COMFORTABLE, THE ENVIRONMENT AFFORDED BY SAN FRANCISCO'S CABLE CARS OFTEN SPARKS LIGHT-HEARTED BANTER BETWEEN STRANGERS.

SOCIAL OPPORTUNITY

Social opportunity enhances not only the quality of our transit journey, but also our lives. The best opportunity for social engagement within public transportation exists when all the planning and design dimensions noted previously are considered and integrated. With proper design and planning, the transit car can overcome the psychological obstacles that inhibit casual interaction. The argument is not that well-designed transit guarantees social engagement or conversation but that it *encourages* it. The likelihood that strangers will engage in conversation is better within a setting that is comfortable, stimulating, and rewarding and where the orientation of seating facilitates eye contact and small talk. Sometimes a third person is needed to catalyze conversation. San Francisco's cable car conductors initiate small talk by mingling with the passengers while collecting fare, announcing stops, and facilitating boarding and alighting. The grips and conductors commonly chat with each other and with other passengers. Even if one chooses not to participate in this casual exchange, there is value simply in listening to others. Some people get information on current events from overhearing a conversation. Some get recommendations on a good book, a movie, or a trendy ethnic restaurant. Tourists provide insight into another culture or place. Ideas and opinions are frequently shared. Information is available to others should they choose to listen.

The cabin within the transit vehicle should permit freedom for active conversation, to allow passengers to express themselves in a friendly manner while instilling a feeling that conversation is appropriate, even encouraged. Like the arrangement of furniture in a room, which can influence behavior and social interaction, the arrangement of the cabin's components—windows, seats, and places for standing, boarding, and exiting, for example—can be arranged to have similar effects. More often than not, opportunities for social interaction within public transit are squandered. An interior arrangement that provides both physical and psychological comfort while facilitating eye contact can engage passengers, promote vivacity, and encourage conversation.

Another important social opportunity aboard public transit can be improved social integration. At one time, American neighborhoods were often comprised of a diverse group of individuals and families. Award-winning journalist Roberta Gratz notes that this social mix was especially characteristic of trolley-car neighborhoods, but that such diversity is rarely seen today. Adults may have kept their social distance when it came to invitations to one another's homes, but neighbors of different color and ethnicity were familiar and often friendly with one another in the neutral territory (i.e., the public realm) of the neighbor-hood sidewalk or shopping street. The kids played together and became friends. That period of residential and social integration is mostly forgot-ten today.[6]

The transit car, however, is one of the few remaining "neutral ter-ritories" where diverse individuals continue to meet one another with regularity and commingle. This wasn't always the case. It is almost incomprehensible that, only a half-century ago, transit passengers in the American South were assigned seats based on the color of their skin. Racial segregation was a shameful period in this nation's history. Today, thankfully, barriers to passenger integration are absent, giving real meaning to the transit creed, "All aboard!"

To ensure that public transit maintains a social mix, the ride must be compelling to people, regardless of age, ethnicity, gender, or, in par-ticular, one's economic station in life. Too often in America, transit riders are wholly comprised of a city's "have-nots." Public transportation needs to appeal to the "haves" of society as well, offering a means of mobility not of necessity but of choice. If transit succeeds in capturing our imagination, elevating our spirits, and promoting friendly banter among a diverse group of individuals, a better, more socially integrated society can result.

ECONOMIC REVITALIZATION

Cities across the nation still struggle with the devastating effects of urban renewal plans that began in earnest in the mid-twentieth century. As retail and housing moved away from the city core, then outside the city limits entirely, many neighborhoods, especially the once-vibrant, mixed-use downtowns, suffered tremendous economic loss. As the new millennium is now under way, American cities are aggressively try-ing to entice merchants and developers to reinvest in their downtowns and historic neighborhoods.[7]

THE DASH—PHOENIX'S DOWNTOWN AREA SHUTTLE—IS PIVOTAL TO THE REVITALIZATION OF THE
COPPER SQUARE DISTRICT. NOT ONLY DO THE SHUTTLE'S GRAPHICS COMPLEMENT THE AREA'S
IMPROVEMENTS AND STRENGTHEN THE IDENTITY OF COPPER SQUARE, BUT THEY REMIND PEOPLE
OF DOWNTOWN'S AMENITIES AND ATTRACTIONS. PERHAPS THE MOST ATTRACTIVE PART OF THE
SHUTTLE IS ITS FARE—IT'S FREE.

The process of attracting private enterprise often begins with public funds, but it can involve private-sector investment, the so-called public-private partnership. This is how Cincinnati is proceeding with its new $132 million streetcar system that will "connect the city's riverfront stadiums, downtown business district and Uptown neighborhoods, which include six hospitals and the University of Cincinnati in a six- to eight-mile loop. Depending on the final financing package, fares may be free, 50 cents, or $1."[8]

Enhancing the pedestrian realm of the neighborhood street—with renovations to facades, street trees, widened sidewalks with bulb-outs at the intersections, human-scaled lighting, benches, and other physical accoutrements—is also an effective strategy in the initial redevelopment or revitalization of an area of the city. In theory, if a place looks appealing and inviting and the city shows interest in its health, safety, and vitality, then merchants will want to do business there, families will want to reside there, and visitors will want to shop and wile away the better part of a day there.

Transit designed to meet the guidelines detailed earlier may prove a valuable contributor to the success of businesses along the transit route. Cars that have a slow, easy pace, with a great deal of transparency and seats that allow better views out to the sidewalk (e.g., Santa Barbara's shuttle), allow riders to survey effortlessly the goods and services along the street. As passengers travel through an area on their way to a destination, a smart dress might catch their eye or they may hear boisterous activity outside a brew pub or inhale the aroma of wood-fired pizza. Those not stopping to patronize these establishments might return the next evening or weekend to do so. All people are potential customers, and it is paramount to the success of businesses that their establishments be freely exposed to passersby, be they on foot, bike, car, or transit. A properly designed transit vehicle not only contributes to the lively, animated scene of a revitalized street or neighborhood, but helps ensure the financial success of that place.

A GREAT GOOD PLACE

This book began with a simple assumption: if the transit car—a public space and, thus, a setting for public life—can provide a rewarding passenger experience, it can more effectively compete against the private automobile for ridership. Alas, skeptics will always maintain that those who can afford to drive will choose private automobiles over public transportation, regardless of the experience offered. Hopefully, the arguments presented within this book will someday prove them wrong. And what about people who are too young or too old to drive? Or those who simply cannot afford to own and operate a car, who rely on public transportation to get them to and from work, their place of worship or study, the hospital or clinic for treatment, and their place of commerce? At the very least, it seems that cities can offer those less privileged a more joyful experience.

Socioeconomic conditions aside, public transportation as a place for personal rejuvenation is real. In his book *The Great Good Place*, Ray Oldenburg praises the "third places" of the built environment and argues for more of them in America. Third places, he contends, provide socially enriching and restorative experiences that the first and second places of home and work cannot. These third places are public gathering spots—such as bookstores, cafés and coffeehouses, bars and taverns, barber shops and beauty salons—where people can put aside the concerns of home and work and rejoice in the comfort of good company. One can expect to find spirited conversation in third places, as well as joy, vivacity, and relief. There are no social restrictions or entry barriers to third places; thus, they serve to expand our personal associations. People of obviously different socioeconomic standings fraternize with one another, simply because it is not one's particular status or station in life that matters in third places but an individual's charm and personality. Unique relationships are found and fostered in such places, allowing individuals to express freely their opinions and swap ideas. Great good places are the heart and soul of a community's vitality, Oldenburg argues, and they help germinate the seeds of democracy.[9]

The Great Good Place is not simply a lengthy praise of socially active gathering spots. Oldenburg's concern "is not so much with the degree of effervescence in the third place spirit as with the factors that combine to make such places almost always pleasant and enjoyable."[10] In other words, once we understand the settings, characteristics, and values of these lively third places, can we—and shouldn't we—create more of them?

Oldenburg did not include the transit car among the many and varied third places of a community. If, however, we approach transportation design as we would our most valued public gathering spots, the transit car has great potential of becoming a great good place.

PREFACE

1. For simplicity and readability, I hereinafter refer to the United States of America as "America" and to its citizens as "Americans," even as "American" refers to places in North, Central, and South America and, to some, the Caribbean.

INTRODUCTION

1. Andres Duany, Elizabeth Plater-Zyberk, and Jeff Speck, *Suburban Nation: The Rise of Sprawl and the Decline of the American Dream* (New York: North Point Press, 2000), 156.

2. Donald Appleyard and Allan Jacobs, "Toward an Urban Design Manifesto," *Journal of American Planning Association*, Vol. 53, No. 1 (1987): 119.

3. Allan B. Jacobs, *Great Streets* (Cambridge: The MIT Press, 1993), 312.

4. Tony Hiss, *The Experience of Place* (New York: Vintage Books, 1991), xiv.

5. See, for example: Tony Hiss, ibid, and, for introductions to the work of J. B. Jackson (also known professionally as John B. and John Brinckerhoff Jackson), Ervin H. Zube, editor, *Landscapes: Selected*

Writings of J. B. Jackson (Amherst: University of Massachusetts Press, 1970), and Helen Lefkowitz Horowitz, editor, *Landscape in Sight: Looking at America* (New Haven: Yale University Press, 1997).

6. See, for example: William H. Whyte, *The Social Life of Small Urban Spaces* (New York: Project for Public Spaces, 1980), and Clare Cooper Marcus and Carolyn Francis, editors, *People Places: Design Guidelines for Urban Open Space* (New York: John Wiley & Sons, 1997).

7. Appleyard and Jacobs, 114.

8. Ibid., 119.

9. Whyte, 19.

CHAPTER ONE

1. Walt Disney's remarks on the day Disneyland opened in Anaheim, California.

2. Tony Hiss, *The Experience of Place* (New York: Vintage Books, 1991), 75.

CHAPTER TWO

1. Christopher Swan, *Cable Car* (Berkeley: Ten Speed Press, 1978), 17.

2. Edgar Myron Kahn, "Andrew Smith Hallidie," The Virtual Museum of the City of San Francisco, sfmuseum.net/bio/hallidie.html, accessed October 15, 2007.

3. Herb Caen, "For Future Reference," Market Street Railway, streetcar.org/mim/spotlight/yesterday/caen/index.html, accessed October 15, 2007.

4. Rudyard Kipling, "In San Francisco," in Alexandra Chapell, editor, *City by the Bay: San Francisco in Art and Literature* (San Francisco: San Francisco Museum of Modern Art, 2002), 56.

5. Herb Caen, *The Cable Car and the Dragon* (San Francisco: Chronicle Books, 1986), unpaginated.

CHAPTER THREE

1. Tennessee Williams, *A Streetcar Named Desire* (New York: Signet, 1951), 70.

2. Roberta Brandes Gratz, with Norman Mintz, *Cities Back from the Edge: New Life for Downtown* (New York: John Wiley & Sons, 1998), 123.

3. Bob Driehaus, "Downtowns Across the U.S. See Streetcars in Their Future," *The New York Times* (August 14, 2008): A17.

4. Williams, 55.

5. William H. Whyte, *City: Rediscovering the Center* (New York: Doubleday, 1988), 119–21.

6. Gratz, 107.

7. [Rick Laubscher], Market Street Railway, "A Brief History of the F-Line Historic Streetcar Service," streetcar.org/mim/streetcars/history/index.html, accessed October 15, 2007.

8. See, for example: Jane Holtz Kay, *Asphalt Nation: How the Automobile Took Over America and How We Can Take It Back* (New York: Crown Publishers, 1997), 213, and Roberta Brandes Gratz, 106.

9. Cliff Slater, "General Motors and the Demise of Streetcars," *Transportation Quarterly*, Vol. 51, No. 3 (Summer 1997): 50.

CHAPTER FOUR

1. Peter Katz, *The New Urbanism: Toward an Architecture of Community* (Black Lake, OH: McGraw-Hill, 1993).

CHAPTER FIVE

1. Chattanooga Area Regional Transportation Authority, "Chattanooga's Electric Bus Story," www.carta-bus.org, accessed September 19, 2005.

CHAPTER SIX

1. From a letter to his brother, Theo van Gogh, August 13, 1888.

2. Email correspondence with the author, April 6, 2005.

3. Jane Holtz Kay, *Asphalt Nation: How the Automobile Took Over America and How We Can Take It Back* (New York: Crown Publishers, 1997), 63. See, also, John A. Jakle and Keith A. Sculle, *The Parking Lot in America: Land Use in a Car Culture* (Charlottesville: University of Virginia Press, in association with the Center for American Places, 2004.)

4. Sewell Chan, "Designing a New Taxicab (But Keeping It Yellow)," *The New York Times* (June 11, 2005): B3.

5. Ibid.

6. Stacie Servetah and Adam Cataldo, "Mayor Bloomberg Orders Taxi Cabs to Be Hybrid by 2012," Bloomberg.com, May 22, 2007, bloomberg.com/apps/news?pid=20601103&sid=aQGO8VgUVowA&refer=us, accessed November 18, 2007.

CHAPTER SEVEN

1. From the article "The 10 Most Beautiful Places in America," *USA Weekend Magazine* (May 18, 2003), Spring Travel section, in which Pittsburgh ranked second.

2. See Franklin Toker, *Buildings of Pittsburgh* (Chicago: Society of Architectural Historians and Santa Fe: The Center for American Places, in association with the University of Virginia Press, 2007), 67.

3. Society for the Preservation of the Duquesne Heights Incline, Pittsburgh, Pennsylvania, "The Duquesne Incline," Society for the Preservation of the Duquesne Heights Incline, incline.pghfree.net, accessed October 15, 2007.

4. Conversation with James Presken, Society for the Preservation of the Duquesne Heights Incline, Pittsburgh, October 6, 2006.

CHAPTER EIGHT

1. Metropolitan Transit Authority, "New York City Transit—History and Chronology," mta.info/nyct/facts/ffhist.htm, accessed October 17, 2007.

2. "Pod cars" may very well be the next chapter written for elevated transit systems in America. Akin to people-movers, pod cars use computer-driven vehicles that glide along elevated tracks, but, instead of shuttling dozens of people as people-movers do, each pod car has a maximum capacity, on average, of just four passengers. Officials in Ithaca, New York, who are considering this technology, cite that pod cars "reduce the need for parking spaces" and offer "more security and privacy than a subway or bus" [as quoted in Michelle York, "Ithaca Takes a Hard Look at Pod Cars," *The New York Times* (September 21, 2008): 33]. These concerns, along with their limited carrying capacity, reveal that pod cars are, perhaps, more an evolution of the private automobile than of public transit.

3. For decades, the Roosevelt Island Tramway was the only commuter aerial tram in the nation. Portland, Oregon, recently completed construction of a commuter aerial tram in December 2006, transporting commuters between the city's South Waterfront district and the Oregon Health & Science University.

4. Anonymous, "Have a Question about Island Operations? Ask RIOC," comment posted August 7, 2006, Roosevelt Island Operating Corporation (RIOC), rioc.com/askcathy2.htm, accessed October 15, 2007.

5. Conversation with the author, September 1, 2006.

6. Roosevelt Island Operating Corporation, "Filming & Photography— Principal Sites," rioc.com/filmsites.htm, accessed October 15, 2007.

7. Conversation with the author, September 2, 2006.

8. Charles Leroux, "The People Have Spoken: Here Are the 7 Wonders of Chicago," *The Chicago Tribune* (September 15, 2005), Tempo Section: 1.

CONCLUSION

1. This remark was recorded by George F. Thompson, on October 2, 1997, at the dedication ceremony of the Cotton Mather Library, when it became part of the nonprofit educational organization now known as the Center for the Study of Place, Inc. The Cotton Mather Library is located in the town of Arthur, Nebraska (population 145), in the beautiful Sand Hills region of the Great Plains.

2. Tony Hiss, *The Experience of Place* (New York: Vintage Books, 1991), 24.

3. Christopher Swan, *Cable Car* (Berkeley: Ten Speed Press, 1978), 10.

4. In New York City, where officials are experimenting with double-decker buses yet again, these vehicles give "riders upstairs a privileged view of the skyscrapers down 34th, then Fifth Avenue, and a sense of majesty, mixed with mild disassociation, above the street-level world scurrying below" [as quoted in April Dembosky, "Double-Decker Bus Tries a Comeback in New York," *The New York Times* (September 9, 2008): C12].

5. It seems difficult to mount a persuasive argument to provide more frequent headways for a transit system that currently faces low ridership. The confounding dilemma circles around operating costs versus passenger convenience. Transit directors argue that it is economically unfeasible to provide shorter headways in the face of paltry passenger demand. Passengers contend that, if transit were more convenient (i.e., more frequent), then more people would ride transit. Jeff Speck, the notable city planner and coauthor of *Suburban Nation: The Rise of Sprawl and the Decline of the American Dream* (2001), provides a persuasive answer to this conundrum. Speck argues: "Transit only attracts large ridership when riders need not consult a schedule before walking to the stop, which means maximum waits of 15 minutes between buses. This is a chicken-and-egg-problem. Current ridership [may] not mandate 15-minute headway service, but such a service would cause ridership to increase to a point where it would begin to make sense. The solution is to start the service with vehicles that are small and efficient enough so that waste is limited. And yes, it must be subsidized publicly, just as our automotive infrastructure is massively subsidized by general taxation revenues. It is time to end the false double standard of "highway investment" vs. "transit subsidy." Both modes of transportation need support, and, today, the smart cities are betting on transit" [as quoted in Jeff Speck, "The City Livable: Modest Proposals for Reviving Downtown" (Report to the citizens of Davenport, Iowa, 2008), 94–95].

6. Roberta Brandes Gratz, with Norman Mintz, *Cities Back from the Edge: New Life for Downtown* (New York: John Wiley & Sons, 1998), 105.

7. See Larry R. Ford, *America's New Downtowns: Revitalization or Reinvention?* (Baltimore: The Johns Hopkins University Press, in association with the Center for American Places, 2003).

8. Bob Driehaus, "Downtowns Across the U.S. See Streetcars in Their Future," *The New York Times* (August 14, 2008): A17.

9. Ray Oldenburg, *The Great Good Place: Cafes, Coffee Shops, Bookstores, Bars, Hair Salons, and Other Hangouts at the Heart of a Community* (New York: Marlowe & Company, 1999).

10. Ibid., 56.

BOOKS

Caen, Herb, *The Cable Car and the Dragon* (San Francisco: Chronicle Books, 1986).

Carter, Graeme, Colin Garratt, David Jackson, Howard Johnston, William D. Middleton, and Karl Zimmerman, *A Guide to Trains: The World's Greatest Trains, Tracks & Travels* (San Francisco: Fog City Press, 2002).

Chapell, Alexandra, editor, *City by the Bay: San Francisco in Art and Literature* (San Francisco: San Francisco Museum of Modern Art, 2002).

Cooper Marcus, Clare, and Carolyn Francis, editors, *People Places: Design Guidelines for Urban Open Space* (New York: John Wiley & Sons, 1997).

Duany, Andres, Elizabeth Plater-Zyberk, and Jeff Speck, *Suburban Nation: The Rise of Sprawl and the Decline of the American Dream* (New York: North Point Press, 2000).

Gratz, Roberta Brandes, with Norman Mintz, *Cities Back from the Edge: New Life for Downtown* (New York: John Wiley & Sons, 1998).

Hilton, George W., *The Cable Car in America* (Palo Alto: Stanford University Press, 1982).

Hiss, Tony, *The Experience of Place* (New York: Vintage Books, 1991).

Jacobs, Allan B., *Great Streets* (Cambridge: The MIT Press, 1993).

Jacobs, Jane. *The Death and Life of Great American Cities* (New York: Random House, 1961).

Katz, Peter, *The New Urbanism: Toward an Architecture of Community* (Black Lake, OH: McGraw-Hill, 1993).

Kay, Jane Holtz, *Asphalt Nation: How the Automobile Took Over America and How We Can Take It Back* (New York: Crown Publishers, 1997).

Lynch, Kevin, *Good City Form* (Cambridge: The MIT Press, 1984).

_____, *The Image of the City* (Cambridge: The MIT Press, 1960).

Oldenburg, Ray, *The Great Good Place: Cafes, Coffee Shops, Bookstores, Bars, Hair Salons, and Other Hangouts at the Heart of a Community* (New York: Marlowe & Company, 1999).

Schrag, Zachary M., *The Great Society Subway: A History of the Washington Metro* (Baltimore: The Johns Hopkins University Press, in association with the Center for American Places, 2006).

Swan, Christopher, *Cable Car* (Berkeley: Ten Speed Press, 1978).

Whyte, William H., *City: Rediscovering the Center* (New York: Doubleday, 1988).

_____, *The Social Life of Small Urban Spaces* (New York: Project for Public Spaces, 1980).

Williams, Tennessee, *A Streetcar Named Desire* (New York: Signet, 1951).

Zube, Ervin H., editor, *Landscapes: Selected Writings of J. B. Jackson* (Amherst: University of Massachusetts Press, 1970).

PERIODICALS AND NEWSPAPERS

Anonymous, "The 10 Most Beautiful Places in America," *USA Weekend Magazine* (May 18, 2003), Spring Travel section.

Appleyard, Donald, and Allan Jacobs, "Toward an Urban Design Manifesto," *Journal of American Planning Association*, Vol. 53, No. 1 (1987): 112–20.

Chan, Sewell, "Designing a New Taxicab (But Keeping It Yellow)," *The New York Times* (June 11, 2005): B3.

Dembosky, April, "Double-Decker Bus Tries a Comeback in New York," *The New York Times* (September 9, 2008): C12.

Driehaus, Bob, "Downtowns Across the U.S. See Streetcars in Their Future," *The New York Times* (August 14, 2008): A17.

Leroux, Charles, "The People Have Spoken: Here Are the 7 Wonders of Chicago," *The Chicago Tribune* (September 15, 2005), Tempo section: 1.

Slater, Cliff, "General Motors and the Demise of Streetcars," *Transportation Quarterly*, Vol. 51, No. 3 (Summer 1997): 45–66.

York, Michelle, "Ithaca Takes a Hard Look at Pod Cars," *The New York Times* (September 21, 2008): 33.

WEBSITES

Anonymous, "Have a Question about Island Operations? Ask RIOC," comment posted August 7, 2006, Roosevelt Island Operating Corporation, rioc.com/askcathy2.htm, accessed October 15, 2007.

Caen, Herb, "For Future Reference," Market Street Railway, streetcar.org/mim/spotlight/yesterday/caen/index.html, accessed October 15, 2007.

Chattanooga Area Regional Transportation Authority, "Chattanooga's Electric Bus Story," CARTA, www.carta-bus.org/CARTA%20Web%20Site/Electric%20Shuttle/CARTA%20Electric%20Bus%20Story.html.

Kahn, Edgar Myron, "Andrew Smith Hallidie," The Virtual Museum of the City of San Francisco, sfmuseum.net/bio/hallidie.html, accessed October 15, 2007.

Market Street Railway, "A Brief History of the F-Line Historic Streetcar Service," Market Street Railway, streetcar.org/mim/streetcars/history/index.html, accessed October 15, 2007.

Metropolitan Transit Authority, "New York City Transit—History and Chronology," MTA, mta.info/nyct/facts/ffhist.htm, accessed October 15, 2007.

NYCabbie, "Dear Cabby," nycabbie.com/dearcabby.html, accessed October 15, 2007.

Rice, Walter and Val Lupiz, "The Cable Car Lady and the Mayor," The Virtual Museum of the City of San Francisco, sfmuseum.org/hist9/cable-car.html, accessed October 15, 2007.

Roosevelt Island Operating Corporation (RIOC), "Filming & Photography—Principal Sites," RIOC, rioc.com/filmsites.htm, accessed October 15, 2007.

"The Duquesne Incline," Society for the Preservation of the Duquesne Heights Incline, incline.pghfree.net/, accessed October 15, 2007.

ACKNOWLEDGMENTS

Jonathan Bennett is a talented writer by any measure. This manuscript is certainly more engaging and readable because of his efforts. In addition to being my impromptu editor, he has been a lifelong friend. Thank you, Jon.

Clare Cooper Marcus, Professor Emeritus of Landscape Architecture at the University of California at Berkeley, gave the initial manuscript a good read and provided inspirational comments. Likewise, Michael Southworth, another respected professor in the College of Environmental Design at the University of California at Berkeley, helped expand my mind while narrowing my focus. The faculty at Cal-Berkeley is second to none, and all in the Design of Urban Places program have influenced this subject matter, particularly Allan Jacobs, Donlyn Lyndon, Peter Bosselmann, and Nezar Al Sayyad.

I owe a debt of gratitude to everyone at the Center for American Places at Columbia College Chicago. George F. Thompson, the Center's gifted publisher, believed in the project, found a series in which this work is a good fit, and has been helpful and encouraging throughout the process. Amber Lautigar and Lenore Lautigar provided assurance and friendly correspondence throughout the manuscript's development. David Skolkin provided a great design and offered excellent technical assistance on the illustrations. And I thank Susan Arritt, a consulting editor for the *My Kind of* series, for her suggested revisions and editorial prowess.

I believe the arguments in the book are stronger because of my many interactions with transit passengers throughout the nation. These personal encounters, which often involved little more than conversations overheard or pleasant chitchat, are supplemented with transit accounts from acquaintances of mine. These accounts gave me better insight into the experience aboard a particular transit system, and, because I think they offer value to the reader as well, they were included in this book. Vivi Bardina provided an excellent synopsis of an emblematic taxicab ride in New York City, and her husband, Derek Nordahl (my brother), provided great photographs and travel accounts aboard the Roosevelt Island Tramway. Linda Roberson has recounted incredible stories of her adventures as a regular commuter aboard San Francisco's cable cars. Often, her commutes to and from work have proven to be the highlights of her day, and, after riding the cable car extensively myself, I can see why.

Selfless transit operators, promoters, and organizers answered many questions, provided photographs and data, and even gave tours to assist in this book's compilation. For information on Seattle's monorail, I thank Glenn Barney, General Manager of Seattle Monorail Services; Kim Pedersen, President of The Monorail Society; Reinhard Krischer, formerly of the Alweg Company; and Rob Kelly, of RAK Productions. Marilyn Amodeo, of Bombardier, provided helpful information on Las Vegas's monorail system. Mark Rothman and Catherine Johnson, both of the Roosevelt Island Operating Corporation, were kind in answering questions regarding New York City's aerial tram, and I offer my gratitude.

The people of Pittsburgh are proud of their funiculars, as well they should be. The system is miraculous, and, while I talked with the many operators, they all expressed a youthful enthusiasm that was certainly contagious. Ruth Miller and Jim Presken, of the Duquesne Incline, were extremely generous and offered literature, tours, and pictures of their fantastic transit system. James Frazier, an operator for the Monongahela

Incline, patiently answered many of my questions while simultane-
ously collecting passenger fares and operating the funicular from his
booth. I know I was a bother, but I could not help myself. It was inspir-
ing just to talk to these people, and I cannot thank them enough for
their graciousness.

Usel is a kindhearted New York City cabbie from Senegal. He
answered many questions about taxicabs, passengers, drivers, and
recent ordinances pertaining to owning and operating cabs in the city.
He taught me a lot about the importance of taxis in New York City and
about the people from around the world who drive them to give their
families better lives here in the United States. While riding in his cab,
Usel unintentionally made me smile. He asked, "So where are you
from?" "San Francisco," I replied. "Oh really! What color are the cabs
out there?" Thanks, Usel.

Finally, I thank James. Of all my encounters with other passengers, both familiar and strange, the one with him had the greatest
effect on this work. I clearly recall that September day in San
Francisco aboard the streetcar with James. With the horrific aftermath
of Hurricane Katrina and London's Underground terrorist bombings
still weighing on everyone's minds, James's story seemed likely to
depress further an already melancholy spirit. Yet his exuberance, wit,
and positive outlook were so infectious I could not help but feel
lighter. He inspires me today, and I suspect he always will. Thank you,
James. Keep the faith.

D arrin Nordahl was born in 1970 in Oakland, California. He completed his bachelor's degree in landscape architecture at the University of California at Davis and his master's degree in urban design at the University of California at Berkeley. Nordahl has taught in the City and Regional Planning Department at UC-Berkeley and in the Landscape Architecture Program at UC-Berkeley Extension.

Interested in a new perspective on city building and design, Nordahl moved to Davenport, Iowa, a once agricultural Rustbelt city now poised to redefine urbanism in the Midwest. He is currently the urban designer for the City of Davenport and operates the municipality's Design Center. His work—a mélange of Left Coast idealism and Midwestern pragmatism—has generated headlines in newspapers and network news stations throughout the Quad Cities. He enjoys life in America's Heartland, along America's great river, the Mississippi, with his wife, Lara, son, Nathaniel, and daughters, Noe and Mia.

ABOUT THE BOOK:

My Kind of Transit was brought to publication in an edition of 2,000 hardcover copies with the generous financial support of the Elizabeth Firestone Graham Foundation, Ray Graham, President, and the Friends of the Center for American Places, for which the publisher is most grateful. The text was set in Akzidenz Grotesk, and the paper is Chinese Goldeast, 128 gsm weight. The book was printed and bound in China. For more information about the Center for American Places at Columbia College Chicago, please see page 176.

FOR THE CENTER FOR AMERICAN PLACES AT COLUMBIA COLLEGE CHICAGO:

George F. Thompson, Founder and Director

Susan Arritt, Series Consulting Editor and Manuscript Editor

Brandy Savarese, Associate Editorial Director

Jason Stauter, Operations and Marketing Manager

Amber K. Lautigar and A. Lenore Lautigar, Associate Editors
    and Publishing Liaisons

Sara E. Lovelace, Editorial Assistant

Marcie McKinley, Design Assistant

David Skolkin, Book Designer and Art Director

Dave Keck, of Global Ink, Inc., Production Coordinator